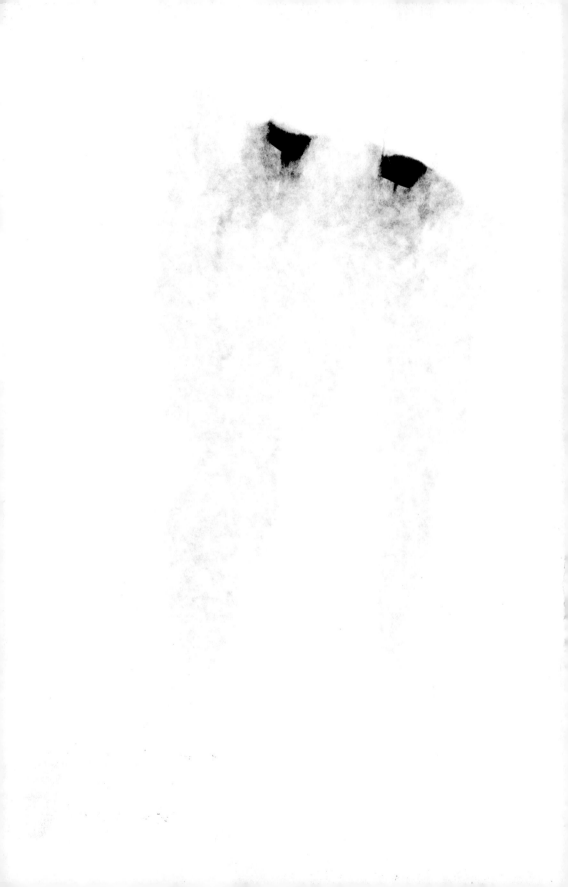

DANICA PATRICK

Racing to History

by J Chris Roselius

Enslow Publishers, Inc.
40 Industrial Road
Box 398
Berkeley Heights, NJ 07922
USA
http://www.enslow.com

Library of Congress Cataloging-in-Publication Data
Roselius, J Chris.
   Danica Patrick : racing to history / J Chris Roselius.
      p. cm. — (Heroes of racing)
   Summary: "A biography of American IndyCar driver Danica Patrick"—Provided by publisher.
   Includes bibliographical references and index.
   ISBN-13: 978-0-7660-3302-3
   ISBN-10: 0-7660-3302-3
   1. Patrick, Danica, 1982—Juvenile literature. 2. Automobile racing drivers—United States—Biography—Juvenile literature. 3. Women automobile racing drivers—United States—Biography--Juvenile literature. I. Title.
   GV1032.P38R67 2009
   796.72092—dc22
   [B]
                                                    2008007695

Printed in the United States of America

10 9 8 7 6 5 4 3 2 1

To Our Readers: We have done our best to make sure all Internet addresses in this book were active and appropriate when we went to press. However, the author and the publisher have no control over and assume no liability for the material available on those Internet sites or on other Web sites they may link to. Any comments or suggestions can be sent by e-mail to comments@enslow.com or to the address on the back cover.

Disclaimer: This publication is not affiliated with, endorsed by, or sponsored by NASCAR. NASCAR®, WINSTON CUP®, NEXTEL CUP, BUSCH SERIES and CRAFTSMAN TRUCK SERIES are trademarks owned or controlled by the National Association for Stock Car Auto Racing, Inc., and are registered where indicated.

♻ Enslow Publishers, Inc. is committed to printing our books on recycled paper. The paper in every book contains between 10% to 30% post-consumer waste (PCW). The cover board on the outside of each book contains 100% PCW. Our goal is to do our part to help young people and the environment too!

Photo credits: AP Photo/Kristie Bull/Graylock.com, 1; AP Photo/Darron Cummings, 6, 46, 79, 90, 96; AP Photo/Indianapolis Star, Gary Mook, 9; AP Photo/Tony Gutierrez, 10, 53; AP Photo/Tom Strattman, 18; AP Photo/John R. Fulton Jr., 22; AP Photo/Tom Strickland, 27; AP Photo/Ed Reinke, 31; AP Photo/Steve Macauley, 34; AP Photo/Mary Altaffer, 36; AP Photo/Greg Giuffrida, 41; AP Photo/Tammie Arroyo, 48; AP Photo/Katsumi Kasahara, 51; AP Photo/Michael Conroy, 62, 83; AP Photo/Marty Lederhandler, 64; AP Photo/Morry Gash, 68–69; AP Photo/Shuji Kajiyama, 105.

Cover Photo: AP Photo/Kristie Bull/Graylock.com.

CONTENTS

BURSTING ONTO THE SCENE

Nearly 300,000 people were on their feet, cheering and screaming. For the second time on May 29, 2005, Danica Patrick was leading the Indianapolis 500, one of the most famous auto races in the world.

Earlier in the race, Patrick claimed the lead on Lap 59, becoming the first female to ever hold the lead in the famed race at Indianapolis Motor Speedway. When she took the lead for a second time, Patrick was only twenty-eight laps from victory. Gambling that her fuel would last until the end of the race, Patrick and her pit crew decided against coming in for a pit stop during a yellow flag. When the eight cars ahead of her came in for more fuel, Patrick vaulted into first place.

"We're going to make this work," engineer Ray Leto told Patrick, urging her to conserve fuel. "Draft that pace car. Steady, steady throttle."[1]

Patrick held the lead from laps 172–175 before Dan Wheldon passed her. Fortune was smiling on Patrick, however, as another caution flag came out. During the caution, engineer Ray Leto told Patrick through the radio, "We need the restart of the twenty-first century here."[2]

With the track cleared and racing set to resume, Patrick timed the restart perfectly and zipped past Wheldon to reclaim first place—once again to the roaring approval of the fans.

Unfortunately for Patrick, the lead would only last four laps. The cars that had decided to pit during the caution period had fresh tires, and perhaps just as important, more fuel. Wheldon chased down Patrick and passed her on Lap 194.

Unable to stay with Wheldon, she was told to conserve her

DID YOU KNOW?

The Indianapolis 500 is a race held every year at the Indianapolis Motor Speedway. Drivers race around the 2.5-mile (4 km) oval track a total of 200 times.

Danica Patrick holds the lead during the running of the 2005 Indianapolis 500.

fuel in an attempt to maintain her position. With Patrick slowing down ever so slightly to make sure she could finish the race, Victor Meira and Bryan Herta passed her on Lap 198. The rookie did not win the race, but she made history with a fourth-place finish, eclipsing the previous best by a female driver, a ninth-place finish by Janet Guthrie in 1978.

"Fantastic job, babe," Leto said. "Sorry we couldn't let you race all the way to the end. Great job coming back from all those problems."[3]

Patrick would have preferred to win the race. That is why she competes. But she knew her finish was an amazing accomplishment for a rookie driver, especially after making several mistakes earlier in the race that could have ended her day early.

"I made a [heck] of a point, are you kidding me?" Patrick said. "I came from the back twice. I was so more content running up front, it was much easier. I think that [what] might have showed the most is that I was able to pass and able to learn how to set someone up better."[4]

LEADING UP TO THE RACE

A blur.

That is all Patrick was on the track at the Indianapolis Motor Speedway during her first practice session in early May. Patrick, the only woman driver in the Indy Racing League in 2005, was an unknown twenty-three-year-old rookie as she prepared for her first Indy 500. Climbing into her No. 16 car for a practice session, she slowly started to build speed as

PATRICK FILE

Height: **5-foot-2**
Weight: **105 pounds**

Date of birth:
March 25, 1982
Beloit, Wisconsin

Childhood home:
Roscoe, Illinois

Resides:
Phoenix, Arizona

Team:
Andretti Green Racing

she zoomed around the two-and-a-half mile (four km) oval.

On that first day of practice, Patrick's speed of 221.463 mph (356 kph) was the fastest among the nine drivers on the track. As the month progressed, she improved with each day of practice, reaching speeds close to 228 mph (367 kph).

Patrick does not stand out in a crowd since she is only five feet, two inches (1.57 meters) tall and barely weighs more than 100 pounds (45 kilograms). While not tall, she has a radiant smile and long, jet-black hair. Patrick became a household name and one of the top stars in the Indy Racing League seemingly overnight.

She appeared on talk shows and was interviewed on nearly every news show imaginable. Reporters surrounded her whenever she was not in her race car, bombarding her with questions and interview requests. In a matter of weeks, Patrick was known around the country and was a media sensation.

"Some of it is she's a very attractive young woman. Some of it's that she's a pretty [darn] good race car driver, as was proven in Japan," Patrick's

DID YOU KNOW?

Because of her fourth-place finish at Indianapolis, Patrick became an overnight media star. She even became the first IndyCar driver in twenty years to be on the cover of *Sports Illustrated*.

Team co-owner Bobby Rahal, left, congratulates Patrick on her fourth-place finish at the 2005 Indy 500.

boss, team co-owner Bobby Rahal, said. "She's the first woman that's really been able to mix it up with the guys."[5]

PROVING HERSELF

Racing fast during practice is one thing, but the pressure increases when it is time to qualify for the Indy 500. On Pole Day, every mistake is increased as the slightest error can cost a driver precious seconds.

Wanting to prove she belonged at Indy, Patrick was almost too anxious and nearly crashed after the green flag dropped. The rear end of her car swung around, but she was able to correct herself and straighten out the car. While she saved herself from a meeting with the wall, the miscue left her with a first lap average speed of 224.920 mph (362 kph).

"She did a really good job of catching her car. That's talent," said fellow racer Tony Kanaan, a Brazilian who finished second at Indy in 2004 en route to the Indy Racing League season title.[6]

Team co-owner Bobby Rahal says Patrick is not afraid to "mix it up" with male drivers.

"I call it nerve," T. J. Patrick, Danica's father, said. "When your car's that loose [turning unpredictably] and you drive that wide-open, that takes a lot of nerve. Not many people can go out there and drive on the edge, knowing there's a good chance they could get really hurt."[7]

With the car back in her control, Patrick zipped around the track and finished with a four-lap qualifying speed of 227.004 mph (365 kph). The time was a historic one. Patrick had the fourth-best qualifying time, the highest qualifying spot ever for a female driver at Indianapolis.

Lyn St. James held the previous record, a sixth-place start in 1994. The showing Patrick put on up to that point in the month was more than Rahal could have envisioned. "I said to her at the start of the year, 'I don't care where you finish. I just want you to fin-ish,'" Rahal said. "I told her I just wanted her to be in a position that when she got to Indy she could have a good month of May."[8]

Due to her record-setting qualifying run, the eyes of the racing world as well as casual fans were

DID YOU KNOW?

Patrick was only twenty-three years old when she competed in the Indy 500. She became the fourth woman to do so, joining Janet Guthrie, Lyn St. James, and Sarah Fisher, who was only nineteen when she made her Indy 500 debut.

now on Patrick. Could the little dynamo actually win one of the most famous races in the world?

The odds were against her. Since the Indy 500 started handing out a rookie-of-the-year award in 1952, only two first-time drivers have won the race. The first was Juan Pablo Montoya in 2000, and Helio Castroneves was the second in 2001. Both drivers, however, were experienced open-wheel drivers. Patrick was new to the Indy Racing League; the Indy 500 was only the fourth IRL race of her career.

Entering the Indy 500, Patrick was showing improvement in each of her three previous races to open the season. After crashing in her debut at Homestead, Florida, Patrick finished fifteenth at Phoenix, twelfth at St. Petersburg, and then fourth at Motegi, Japan. In that race, Patrick qualified second and held the lead for thirty-two laps.

SHE SAID IT

"In this society these days, women are widely accepted in all kinds of cross-gender areas. So, yeah, it's time."

— Danica Patrick

"All the ingredients are in place," Janet Guthrie, the first woman to compete in the Indy 500, said before the 2005 Indy 500. "Patrick is the first woman to arrive at the Speedway with top-notch equipment and the full backing of a winning team. And she has the talent and determination to make the most of her opportunity. Despite her inexperience at Indianapolis, there's no reason Patrick can't win if she gets the right breaks on race day."[9]

OVERCOMING HER MISTAKES

Obviously, Patrick did not get the right breaks on race day. Not heading to pit lane helped her grab the lead near the end of the race, but ultimately the lack of fuel and fresh tires kept her out of Victory Lane.

Several other mishaps slowed Patrick during the race as well. Her first mistake came soon after she claimed the lead for the first time on Lap 59, when she stalled her car in the pits. Entering pit row in fourth place, her forty-eight-second pit stop dropped her to sixteenth place.

On Lap 155, Patrick went into a spin and clipped fellow driver Tomas Enge. The left-front wing was torn off Patrick's car and the nose cone was damaged, forcing her to pit and have repairs made. The trouble dropped her back into the pack once again.

Never losing focus, Patrick overcame the mistakes, weaving and darting her way through the field and to the front of the pack. She kept her poise and never lost sight of her goal, which was to drive the best race possible and try to earn a win. Patrick fell short of winning the race, but her performance on the track earned her the rookie of the year honor.

"She's going to be here more times to achieve that," said Patrick's mother, Bev. "I'm just thinking about it more as her being a rookie. It was just her sixth oval start, and she adapted well to it."[10]

GROWING UP
IN ILLINOIS

Danica Sue Patrick was born to race. Her parents, T. J. and Bev, were snowmobile-racing enthusiasts. The two met in the 1970s, while T. J. was entering snowmobile races as a driver and Bev worked as a mechanic for another snowmobile driver. T. J. was very successful as a snowmobile racer, and won a title in 1978.

Her parents owned a few businesses in their hometown of Roscoe, Illinois. One business was a plate-glass company, and another was a coffee shop in town. On March 25,

1982, Danica was born in Beloit, Wisconsin. Two years later, her sister, Brooke, was born.

Danica did standard childhood things, such as playing with dolls or dressing up like a cheerleader for fun. Additionally, she was always very athletic and determined to succeed during her childhood. She loved to be challenged. It became apparent that she wouldn't back down from anyone or anything, much like her personality as an adult.

"She was feisty, [and] it's kind of funny how that played out," fifth-grade teacher Mike Rhines said.[1]

Carol Allen, Danica's third-grade teacher, recalls Danica's "snapping black eyes. Even though she was little, nobody got anything over on her."[2]

THE ACCIDENTAL RACER

Danica may never have become a race car driver if not for Brooke. At the age of eight, Brooke wanted to try her hand in go-kart racing. Because of their backgrounds, T. J. and Bev enthusiastically embraced Brooke's decision.

Not wanting to be left out, Danica wanted to give racing a try as well. Brooke learned that racing was not in her blood, especially after crashing four times in one race. Living on the edge was not her idea of fun.

Danica, however, was fascinated with racing and everything it involved. She could not get enough of the sport and was soon competing in races organized by the World Karting Association. Danica didn't let failure stop her, even after brake problems led her to crash into a building in her debut.

DID YOU KNOW?

Like Patrick, many famous drivers got their starts racing go-karts. NASCAR champions Jeff Gordon and Tony Stewart both gained experience in go-kart racing, as did seven-time Formula One champion Michael Schumacher.

"The first day Danica got into a go-kart, she totaled it out," T. J. Patrick said. "The first thing she wanted to know was when we were getting a new one."[3]

In Danica's first race, six laps into the competition, the race leader lapped her.

"I couldn't even keep up on the parade laps," Danica said.[4]

Nothing would stop Danica from becoming a top driver. According to her, racing was what she was supposed to do in life.

"At age ten, I had found my life's passion. From that point forward, I had a one-track mind," Danica wrote in her autobiography, *Danica: Crossing the Line*. "Instead of playing soccer after school or taking piano lessons, I dedicated myself to becoming the best race car driver in the world."[5]

Her choice of racing cars raised some eyebrows. First, of course, was the stereotype of a woman racing a car. But some worried that Danica would be injured racing go-karts, especially since she wasn't as big as many of the other drivers. In typical Danica fashion, she brushed off such worries.

Patrick began competing in World Karting Association events in 1993. She finished fourth in one series of races and second in another. In 1994, she won her first national points title and she added titles in 1995 and 1996.

"There's a heck of a lot more cheerleading injuries than anything else and I was a cheerleader," she said. "It looks like I have a thing for dangerous sports, don't I? It's part of the game. You have just as much potential for injury riding down the street. I was put here for one reason. And that's to drive race cars."[6]

Danica dedicated herself to improving her concentration on the track and improving her skills behind the wheel of the go-kart. The ability to see instant success drove her to become better and better on the track. Her father could see the improvement each and every week as well. "I'd go around the track in maybe 52 seconds, and then I'd come in and say, 'Was that

Patrick's passion for racing go-karts as a child turned into a love of open-wheel racing as an adult.

51?'" Danica said. "Dad would say, 'Yeah, it's 51 now.' It was that setting out to go faster and doing it; seeing the improvement that was so satisfying and confidence-building. It was, 'OK, let's do 50; let's do 49, 48.' I just got attracted to it."[7]

FULL FAMILY SUPPORT

By the end of her first season in 1992, she finished second in the points standings out of twenty drivers in her age group. The following year she entered more races and by the age of twelve she won her first Grand National Championship. Praise was awarded to Danica for winning, but she is quick to credit her father.

"My dad was the one with the knowledge," Patrick commented. "He knew how to prepare a go-kart and how to make it go fast. He knew about clutches and carburetors. He just knew what to do."[8]

DID YOU KNOW?

In 1997, Patrick won the World Karting Association Grand National Championship HPV Class and won the WKA Grand National Championship in the Yamaha Lite class.

She continued to progress as a driver, with each race teaching her something new, like handling turns better or positioning herself better on the track in order to pass an opponent. Over the next several years, she won two more national titles and ten regional titles.

In 1996, she won thirty-nine of the forty-nine races she entered.

Each race Danica won was a win for the entire family. Bev and T. J. were there every step of the way. They acted as her pit crew and engineering team. They were her fan club and sponsor. Brooke was, and still is, her biggest fan. Danica wanted to become the best driver, and her parents did all they could to make sure that dream came true.

DID YOU KNOW?

While in high school, Patrick was very active in extracurricular activities. She was a cheerleader and she also participated in volleyball and basketball. She also had an interest in music. She was in the school choir and the band.

"We put our lives on hold pursuing her dream," T. J. Patrick says. "We didn't have family vacations or things because we were supporting her. We had to go to work to pay for her racing."[9]

LEARNING FROM THE PROFESSIONALS

Danica knew her future was not in go-kart racing but behind the wheel of an open-wheel race car. In order to ever get into one of those cars, she needed to learn more about the sport and what it takes to succeed.

She started to attend a driving school run by Lyn St. James, who helped open the door for female

Lyn St. James operated a driving school that Patrick attended, and introduced Patrick to the world of racing.

drivers in open-wheel racing and competed in the Indy 500 several times. St. James easily recognized that Danica had the determination and skill needed to be a successful driver.

"It's hard to put into words, but there's just another level that you're looking for with drivers," St. James says. "She had an intensity that is unusual for someone that age."[10]

St. James helped groom the young Danica, introducing her to important people in the racing world.

James even took her to the 1997 Indy 500, allowing Danica to see firsthand what it takes to win on the highest level of racing.

"Out of 200 that have gone through my program, no more than ten set themselves apart that I've gone out of my way to help behind the scenes," St. James said. "They have to be exceptional. It's not good enough to just be good. The reality is you have to be extraordinary. I saw Danica as extraordinary."[11]

Eventually, Danica received her first big break. Some racing officials spotted her talent as a go-kart racer. They mentioned that she should head to England, where she could improve her skills against some of the best young drivers from around the world in the British developmental racing series.

With the backing of her parents and some help from sponsors, Danica left for England at the age of sixteen.

APPRENTICESHIP IN ENGLAND

It is hard for any parent to see their child leave home. But Danica wasn't just leaving the security of her childhood house; she was going across the Atlantic Ocean to race in England. It wasn't easy, but Danica had the full backing of her family.

"My family is 110 percent supportive of what I do," Danica said. "They would be crushed as I would if I didn't make it as a racing driver."[1]

Bev and T. J. Patrick understood the decision, and knew it was the right one to make for their sixteen-year-old. "If you want to be the best lawyer, you go to Harvard," said Bev Patrick. "If you want to be the best driver, you go to England."[2]

Danica and her family were able to arrange some sponsorships to help defray the cost, though T. J. and Bev had to come up with most of the money to support their daughter. In 1998, Patrick left Hononegah Community High School in Rockton, Illinois—she later earned her General Education Degree—and went to England, where she experienced both turmoil and elation.

BECOMING AN OUTSIDER

Drivers from Europe and South America regularly head to England to prove themselves. But those drivers are often male. Patrick was a young female from America trying to prove herself in a man's world.

"Running my first lap in England was such a thrill," Danica said. "Because I knew it was a big step and

DID YOU KNOW?

Patrick made a major decision in her life at the age of sixteen. She was invited to race in the Formula Vauxhall Series in Europe. Patrick wanted to become a better driver on the track, but driving in the series meant moving to England. With her parents' permission, Patrick dropped out of high school and moved to Milton Keynes, England.

the beginning of my future."[3] What she did in go-karts in the United States didn't matter on the tracks in England. Patrick understood she was in a whole new world. "It was my college," Danica said. "England is great for racing, like Harvard is great for law."[4]

Danica, however, wasn't welcomed with open arms. During her first two months there, she slept on a couch that belonged to a woman who worked for Jaguar. When Danica was able to get her own place, it was exceptionally small.

When she was at the track, she was often alone. Few of the other drivers would talk to her, or even acknowledge her. When she succeeded on the track by running the fastest laps, managers of other teams would ask their drivers why a girl was beating them.

Team co-owner Bobby Rahal, left, provided Patrick with support early in her career.

"All the drivers hung out together, and I was left out of the equation a lot. They wouldn't call me," Danica said. "It was boys being boys."[5]

While she was pursuing her dream, Danica missed her family. She did all she could to fit in with the other drivers. She made some friends, but for the most part she was always an outsider. She also

CROSSING THE LINE

Patrick wrote an autobiography several years ago, describing her life leading up to and shortly after her initial run in the Indy 500. In the book, *Danica: Crossing the Line*, she talks about her time in England.

While there, she went through some tough times and started to do things that were bad for her health, such as drinking alcohol. The fun and fast times, however, nearly derailed her career. At one point, she was told to grow up and become more responsible or else she would lose her sponsorship.

She quickly realized the mistake she was making. She stopped drinking and dedicated herself to her sport.

"It made me a much tougher person," Patrick said. "It also made me more closed off. I became less open about some things. I learned not to talk about everything that was on my mind or all the things going on in my personal life."[6]

Patrick said she resents those years in England at times because of the separation from family and friends. But she also knows the experience she had there helped her become the determined person she is today—a responsible adult.

experienced rejections from boyfriends. In an attempt to fit in, she often headed to the pubs after practice and attended parties, all with no adult supervision.

Coming home to visit after the 1999 driving season, Danica was fifteen pounds heavier than when she left, due to her vices. Her personality was also different. She wasn't the happy little girl who left for England full of hopes and dreams. Instead, she was a little distant and guarded.

She realizes she made some poor choices. But Danica also realizes the experience helped make her a stronger person. Danica said she grew up very quickly while in England, learning as much about life as cars.

"I know that England changed me a bit," she said. "I know I became a little bit colder, a little different. When I came home every six months, my parents said, 'You're different. You're a different person.' I said, 'I'm sorry, but you sent me there.' What doesn't kill you makes you stronger. It was tough, but it's made me what I am today. I hope people like it. If they don't, this is me. I'm very true to myself and true to my personality."[7]

SUCCESS ON THE TRACK

Struggling to fit in away from the track, Danica had no trouble showing what she could do on the track. She had a brief run in the 1998 Formula Vauxhall Winter Series before running for a full season in 1999.

Despite not always getting the support other drivers were getting from engineers and often racing with inferior equipment, Danica placed ninth in the final 1999 points standings. That result would have been outstanding for any seventeen-year-old. But since it was a young American girl placing ninth, racing officials started to take notice of her.

Danica was proving she had the talent to compete. In 2000, she increased her level of competition. Danica competed in the European Formula Ford Series and was a test driver for the Mygale factory team as part of Haywood Racing. But she really made her mark by racing in the more competitive British Zetek Formula Ford Series. The series is considered one of the toughest racing series in the world.

"I knew if I was going to reach goals like Formula One or CART Champ Cars I needed to race in British Formula Ford," she said. "The series has some of the best wheel-to-wheel racing in the world. I knew I would improve my skills by racing in that series."[8]

Danica drove for Andy Welch Racing and received more support than she had in 1999. During the season, the team didn't always get the results they expected—until the biggest race of the year, the Formula Ford Festival.

In a race with a long history, Danica started in ninth and was the lone woman in the field of twenty-eight drivers. What she did was unprecedented. Weaving her way through the field like a veteran driver, Danica zipped past fellow drivers.

She made one daring pass after another. If another driver made a mistake, Danica quickly took

After her stint on a couple of racing circuits in England, Patrick was well prepared for the IndyCar Series.

advantage. When the checkered flag dropped, she was in second place, missing a victory by only half a second.

That second-place finish was the highest ever by a female driver in the event's history. It matched the highest-ever finish by an American driver, equaling the finish of former Indy 500 winner and CART champion Danny Sullivan in 1974.

Her jaw-dropping performance drew worldwide attention. She received letters and phone calls from some of the most influential people in the sport, such as Formula One president Bernie Ecclestone, three-time CART series champion Bobby Rahal, and McLaren Racing's Ron Dennis.

"A lot of people said it was the surprise result of the event," Danica said. "But I almost expected it after making a lot of progress during the year and driving so well over that weekend. I think it was a bit of a relief rather than anything."[9]

Danica mesmerized Rahal. He understood the trials and tribulations the young driver experienced during her time in England. He believed that if she could succeed there, she could succeed on any level of racing. "England is the motor racing equivalent of a street fight," Rahal says. "If you can go over there

DID YOU KNOW?

In 1998, Patrick made her debut in the Formula Vauxhall Series at the age of sixteen. In 1999, Patrick finished ninth in the Formula Vauxhall Championship in Great Britain. The next year, she finished second at the Formula Ford Festival in England, the highest-ever finish for an American driver.

and compete in that atmosphere, it really speaks volumes not only about your talent but also your determination."[10]

CHANGE IN LUCK

Coming off her fantastic result in the Ford Festival, Patrick was excited about the 2001 season. But nothing went as planned for her that year. Haywood Racing provided her with a Mygale car, but the car didn't conform well to Patrick's driving style. According to David Henderson, who worked for Haywood Racing, Patrick was not as aggressive as the other drivers.

"She was very smooth," recalled Henderson. "The car really needed to be taken by the scruff of the neck. She did a good job, but the car wasn't what we hoped it would be. It hampered her more than the others because of her driving style."[11]

Ford Motor Company believed the money that was supposed to go to Patrick was possibly being used for other drivers on the team instead. They believed she may not have been receiving the best engineers or support. But Patrick continued to race and do well, and she continued to be watched by Rahal.

"It really impressed me that at such a young age she would leave home and go to live in England," said Rahal, who raced in England when he was younger. "That spoke volumes about her commitment. A lot of young people say they want to be race car drivers, but not many are willing to do the things you have to do.

"And I have to tell you it's not easy for an American to live in that society. Certainly I think, let's face it, motor racing has not been the most open for the female gender and particularly in England. So all of those things just, in my mind, spoke volumes about her commitment and dedication to what she wanted to achieve."[12]

Ford eventually terminated Patrick's run in England, feeling she wasn't getting the support she needed. Patrick, meanwhile, felt it was time to head back to the United States anyway. She felt she had proved she could compete with the best.

"After racing in Europe, I received a lot of experience that can help me get to the top of the sport. I just need the chance to show my abilities."[13]

Patrick didn't have to wait long to get the chance she was looking for. Impressed with her character and her skills, in 2002 Rahal signed Patrick to a multiyear contract to race for the Rahal Letterman team. The team is co-owned by Rahal and late-night talk show host David Letterman.

Patrick was coming back to America.

DID YOU KNOW?

While driving in Europe, Patrick's skill caught the attention of former CART champion and Indy 500 winner Bobby Rahal, who was a co-owner of Rahal Letterman Racing with late-night TV host David Letterman. Patrick agreed to a three-year contract with Rahal Letterman in 2002.

Talk show host David Letterman, right, joined Bobby Rahal's team as an owner in 1996.

Three years in England was long enough for Patrick to gain the experience she felt she needed. She encountered success on the track, as shown with her second-place finish in the Formula Ford Festival.

Patrick headed home in 2001. That year, she won the Gorsline Scholarship Award as the top upcoming road-racing driver. Patrick was recognized as the top female open-wheel driver with international experience. The only problem was, she did not have a sponsor yet. She was a

Once lacking any sponsors, Patrick now has plenty of support.

driver without a car and spent nearly every waking moment going to races and talking to whoever would listen, in search of a sponsor.

DID YOU KNOW?

Before joining the Indy Racing League for Rahal Letterman, Patrick gained more experience driving in the Barber Dodge Pro Series in 2002, finishing seventh in her first race and fourth three weeks later. In 2003, she moved up one level to the Toyota Atlantic Series and became the first woman to earn a podium finish when she placed third at the Monterrey Grand Prix in Mexico. In the season finale, she placed second and finished the season with five top-five finishes, ranking sixth.

"Every weekend we would go somewhere else and try to get noticed," T. J. Patrick says. "Of course she got discouraged, but she knew something would happen eventually. It was just a matter of time."[1]

The search didn't last long thanks to Rahal, who signed Patrick to race for his team, which was known as Team Rahal Racing at the time before it became Rahal Letterman Racing. In signing Patrick, Rahal let everyone know that he had high expectations from his new driver.

"Danica has that chip on her shoulder that all champion drivers need to make it," Rahal wrote in the foreword of Patrick's autobiography. "She's not fearful or unwilling to face any challenge. She not only wants the challenge, she looks for it. That is what champions do. They are not afraid and they don't shy from difficult times. They go through life with a bring-it-on attitude. In addition, it is that 'C'mon, take a shot at me' thinking that spurs her confidence and allows her to sustain a challenge and come back harder. It's what I call fire in the belly. It's a hunger and need to be the best. That is Danica."[2]

Before Patrick could begin her career in the Indy Racing League, however, Rahal wanted his young driver to gain more experience in the United States, where there are more races on oval tracks than road races.

So Patrick competed in the Barber Pro Series in a limited schedule in 2002, competing in five races. She then competed in the Toyota Atlantic Series, a top developmental open-wheel racing series, in 2003. Rahal expected nothing but success from Patrick.

"What impressed me from Day 1 is when she went to England at 16 because that's the toughest environment and every young gun in the world is over there," the three-time CART champion said. "She had the hunger and dedication to succeed and she went toe-to-toe with those guys. She's a racer, and I think she'll do just fine."[3]

Rahal knew about Patrick and her early struggles in England. But he also knew she was held to a different standard as a female than if she were a male. Patrick demonstrated she was able to change by cleaning up her life while still oversees, but Rahal made sure she would remain focused while racing for his team.

"When she got back over here, we had talks about how it had to be," said Rahal, who told Patrick: "You have to change the way you're living.

"Initially, she thought it was unfair. Well, life's unfair. She lives in a fishbowl. That's unfortunate, but that's her reality. I think that's why she was so private about her life when she made it."[4]

While Rahal was always a big supporter of Patrick, signing her to a contract wasn't very easy.

Patrick's background was in road racing due to her time in England. Because of that, she was looking at possibly signing a contract with a Champ Car team, which would allow her to race on more road courses.

But the IRL had two things to its advantage when Rahal was trying to convince Patrick to sign with his team. First, the league was going to add two road races and a street show in 2005. Second, one of

DID YOU KNOW?

Patrick excelled in 2004 in the Toyota Atlantic Series. In ten of the twelve races she entered, she finished in the top five. She was the only driver to complete every lap of every race. She finished third in the points standings with 269 points.

Patrick's experience on road courses was one of the reasons she decided to leave England for the IRL.

the IRL races is the Indy 500, the biggest open-wheel race in the United States.

"Honestly, when I left England and hadn't made any F-1 inroads, I thought I hadn't made the highest level and then I realized it doesn't have to be like that," said Patrick. "I want to be happy racing and I want to have fun racing and be around family and friends."[5]

Rahal said he used the fact that the IRL competes in the Indy 500 and that it added three road races to convince Patrick to sign with him.

"The IRL has the Indy 500 and I don't care what other races you win, everything else pales in comparison," said Rahal, who won the Indy 500 as a driver in 1986.[6]

Once the deal was complete, Patrick was ecstatic to be a part of Rahal racing. "I'm very confident and I'm a good driver with a good team," Patrick declared.[7]

GETTING STARTED

Patrick's first race for Team Rahal in the Barber Dodge Pro Series came in Toronto in July. The twenty-year-old got her feet wet during qualifying, when she recorded the sixteenth-fastest time in the No. 89 car owned by the Team Rahal/Rahal Automotive Group.

DID YOU KNOW?

In 2004, Patrick became the first female driver to win a pole position in the Toyota Atlantic Series when she claimed the pole in Round Five in Portland, Oregon.

Her finish could have been better. She was as fast as fifth early in the round and was in the top ten for most of qualifying before tire trouble slowed her down. She also spun the car around.

"I'm a little frustrated with myself today. I think I was expecting to come out fast after the Sebring test with the Barber Dodge car. But I quickly realized that the street course is much different than Sebring,"

Patrick said. "It was tough getting a consistency in the chassis setup."[8]

In the second qualifying round, the crew made some changes to the setup of the car. Patrick took advantage and qualified eleventh and then went out and finished seventh in her first race.

Three weeks later, Patrick put on her best show in Vancouver. After several solid rounds of qualifying, she placed fourth, her best finish during her stint in the Barber Dodge Pro Series.

In the 2002 Long Beach Grand Prix Toyota Pro/Celebrity Race, Patrick captured the pole and won the pro division, beating former Trans Am champion Tommy Kendall and IRL driver Sarah Fisher.

MOVING UP A LEVEL

With her apprenticeship in the Barber Dodge series done, Patrick raced in the Toyota Atlantic Championship series in 2003 and 2004. Once again, she showed off her talent to the rest of the racing world.

In 2003, she claimed a pair of podium results (a top-three finish) and recorded five top-five finishes as a rookie.

Her third-place showing in Monterrey, Mexico, in March made Patrick the first female to earn a podium finish in the thirty-year history of the Atlantic series. Her best result came in the season finale in

Miami, when she placed second. Overall, she finished sixth in the points standings for the season.

In 2004, Patrick continued to do well in the series. She was the only driver to complete every lap and she became the first female driver to win a pole position in the series when she claimed the top spot in round five at Portland. She ended up finishing second in the race and she added third-place finishes at Monterrey and Cleveland. For the season, she ended third in the points standings with 269 points, and she had ten top-five finishes in twelve races.

But the best news of all for Patrick in 2004 was Rahal's decision to have Patrick race in the IRL starting in 2005. He felt his young driver was more than ready for the top level. His announcement, however, took Patrick somewhat by surprise, since she would become only the fourth woman ever to compete in the IRL.

"I had no idea Bobby was going to say that. . . . It was one of those moments when you pinch yourself to make sure you heard what you just heard. It was my dream come true."[9]

Said Rahal: "Believe me, I never would have put her in this car if I thought she was going to make a fool out of herself or us. She's under a lot of pressure here, but she can handle it."[10]

ROOKIE OF THE YEAR

As twenty-two drivers were getting ready to qualify for slots in the Toyota Indy 300 at Homestead-Miami Speedway in 2005, one driver was already garnering attention. That driver was Danica Patrick, the rookie in the No. 16 Argent Mortgage car for Rahal Letterman Racing.

Since first climbing into a go-kart at the age of ten and then going through the rigors of racing in England as a teenager, Patrick had waited a lifetime for this moment.

"I've never been in this situation before," Patrick said of the butterflies she was feeling ahead of her first race in South Florida. "I'm nervous for sure but I want to get going. The real challenge begins when the season starts."[1]

As the season started, Patrick wasn't just a rookie, however. She was also the lone female driver. She was prepared for the comparisons to previous female drivers such as Lyn St. James, Janet Guthrie, and Sarah Fisher. They are the only three other women to have ever driven in the Indy 500. But all Patrick wanted was to be compared to her fellow drivers, male or female.

"Comparisons with [other woman drivers] don't affect me at all. I can only do the best I can," Patrick said before the start of the season. "The things they've done helped others come in to the business but at the end of the day I'm just another driver with expectations and goals."[2]

Patrick said she had several simple goals entering her rookie season. The first was to remain confident in her skill and ability. She also wanted to learn during each and every race and not get too excited or disappointed throughout the course of the season.

The biggest adjustment for Patrick, however, was the length of the races in the Indy Racing League. The Toyota Atlantic Championship was basically a series of sprint races that lasted less than an hour. In the IRL, races are routinely 300 miles (482.8 km) and sometimes as long as 500 miles (804.6 km).

In preparation for the 2005 season, Patrick spent a lot of time with Paul Hospenthal, who is a physical trainer and now her husband.

"My fiancé is teaching me how to be fit and we're working with heavier weights in our strength training," she said. "I've learned to keep the sessions regular and keep a good eye on my blood sugar."[3]

LET THE RACING BEGIN

Patrick started her rookie campaign with a ninth-place starting position after a fine qualifying round at Homestead. The race, however, didn't go as planned, as Patrick was knocked out on Lap 158 due to an eight-car accident. She sustained a concussion in the accident.

From left, Milka Duno, Sarah Fisher, Lyn St. James, and tennis great Billie Jean King pose with Patrick.

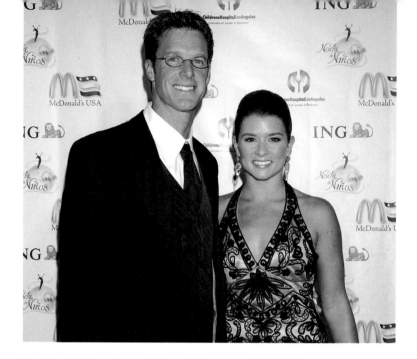

Patrick's husband, Paul Hospenthal, left, works as a physical therapist.

"I had a lot of fun while I was out there," Patrick said. "The car was great, but I was just trying to be patient and get a feel for the race. Sunday was the longest race of my career, and since it was only my 12th day in an IndyCar, I wanted to gain as much experience as possible and increase my comfort level. Going into the race, I just wanted to finish. Every lap I run in an IndyCar is experience, and that experience is going to pay benefits later in the season. I really don't remember the accident, but I know we were having a pretty decent race for our first time out. I just wish I could have finished."[4]

Two weeks later in Phoenix, Patrick struggled during qualifying, earning a starting position of

IT MUST BE LOVE

After the 2005 season, Patrick got married to Paul Hospenthal, a physical therapist she met in 2001. She met him not long after her experience in England, where she allowed only those she really trusted to get close to her.

But Hospenthal had a certain confidence about him that allowed Patrick to feel relaxed around him. A relationship that started as a friendship soon became one in which they were unable to be apart. They were married on November 19, 2005, and Patrick says her relationship with Hospenthal is what defines her now.

"She's made a 180-degree (turnaround)," said her father. "She leans on Paul a lot. He's her sounding board."[5]

Hospenthal, who is almost seventeen years older than Patrick, has watched his wife change her behavior since they became a couple and now husband and wife.

"She's always thinking about how can she make my day better, whether that's ironing my clothes, fixing me breakfast, packing my lunch or running the errands that I need done," he said.

"Our relationship is easy like that. It's comfortable."[6]

Hospenthal has helped Patrick in a variety of areas. He does what he can to caution her against doing too much promotion too soon, or at the wrong time, which can lead to unintended consequences.

He also tries to stay out of the spotlight, knowing that she is the person fans want to meet and talk to, not him. One thing that he has not changed about Patrick, however, is her inability to bite her tongue at times.

"He's a very smart, calculated man," she said. "When he says something, he's sure it'll come out right because he's already thought it out. My mouth just opens."[7]

eighteenth. While she was able to finish the race, she didn't overtake many other drivers as she placed fifteenth. She followed with a twelfth-place showing in St. Petersburg, Florida. The finish was somewhat disappointing considering it was a street race.

The 2005 season started to turn around in Motegi, Japan. Racing at Twin Ring Motegi, Patrick had her best showing yet in both qualifying and during the race. During qualifying, she turned in a lap of 204.502 mph (329 kph), good enough for a pole position. However, eleven more drivers still were waiting for their turns.

In the end, Sam Hornish Jr. earned the pole position, but Patrick still was starting in second.

"I was so mad when we lost the pole because we were so close," said Patrick, who became the first female since Sarah Fisher at Richmond in 2003 to start on the front row. "I still have a lot to learn."[8]

Patrick continued her fine racing form during the race the next day. Pursued

DID YOU KNOW?

Constantly trying to juggle her time, Patrick needed help to keep her life in order. That is why she is so quick to credit Rahal Letterman Racing's public relations department for helping her manage her schedule.

Not only did it help set up her interviews with the media, it also scheduled time for haircuts, pedicures, and facials.

Holding press conferences after races helps Patrick maintain her visibility to the public.

throughout the race, she held off most of the competition en route to placing fourth, her best finish of the
season. The confidence she gained in Japan carried
over to her next race—the Indy 500.

She was nearly at the top of her game throughout the month during qualifying, earning a fourth-
place start and the attention of fans and media from
around the globe. Patrick finished fourth in the race
and even held the lead late in the race.

MORE SUCCESS TO COME

After the 2005 Indy 500, the media besieged Patrick,
since she was the first woman to ever hold the lead in

the Indy 500 and had the best-ever finish by a female driver. Patrick, however, was able to maintain her focus on her job.

The next race sent the drivers to Fort Worth, Texas, and the Texas Motor Speedway. Patrick's crew continued their impressive work with the car as she posted the third-best qualifying time. Once again, Patrick was starting on the first or second row. Her good fortune didn't carry over in the race, however, as she finished thirteenth. She then placed tenth the following race at Richmond Motor Speedway.

Patrick turned things around at the Argent Mortgage Indy 300 at Kansas Motor Speedway. The rookie became only the second female in series history to win a pole when she turned in a lap of 214.668 mph (345 kph).

The pole position, however, didn't turn into a victory. Patrick had to battle her car, poor pit stops and traffic for much of the race. She was able to climb to fifth place on Lap 182, but she had to come into pit row one more time for some fuel. The pit helped lead to a ninth-place finish.

"It felt good to lead on that first lap but I think our fifth gear wasn't quite fast enough," said Patrick, who had her second consecutive top-ten finish and her fourth in five races. "So I moved into the middle of the pack and tried to stay with the leaders. Overall, we

Despite her groundbreaking achievements at the 2005 Indy 500, Patrick was able to stay focused.

made the car faster through the day but it was frustrating when we dropped back a couple of times. The wind was a problem for everybody out there today and that caused my car to develop a push. But the car was pretty good in most cases and we were able to come back towards the leaders late in the race."[9]

Patrick was solid again in the following race, placing seventh after placing second in qualifying.

Unfortunately, the following three weeks were a disaster. She was knocked out of the race in Milwaukee due to an accident on Lap 125, leaving her with a nineteenth-place finish. She then placed twentieth in Michigan due to mechanical trouble. After winning the pole in Kentucky, she struggled the next day during the race and ended up placing sixteenth.

The rest of the season unfolded the same way the first twelve races did. Patrick had two more top-ten finishes and won her third pole position at

SHE SAID IT

"I think my first highlight of the year probably came at Homestead when I was finally understanding, learning, being more brave in the race with passing, not just on the inside but on the outside, too. I went three-wide down in turns three and four and went around two cars. I was the third one on the top. That still scares me to this day, being three-wide and being the one furthest out. That was a highlight for me. It was a brave moment.

"Obviously, Indianapolis was good. I think qualifying—actually, another highlight would have been Motegi, almost getting on pole. I went from not really being anywhere in qualifying to I think Sam Hornish was like one of the last couple to go. I was on pole all the way up until the last guy. That felt really good. That was a good moment."

— Danica Patrick

Chicagoland Speedway. But she also was knocked out of two races due to accidents and placed eighth, sixth, and sixteenth in the three races she did finish. The end result was a season in which she won the Bombardier Rookie of the Year Award. While she didn't win a race, she had seven top-ten finishes and her three poles tied for the most in the IRL.

FOCUS OF ATTENTION

Despite the up-and-down season, Patrick was one of the most popular drivers in the IRL. She was a magnet when it came to attention. Fans lined up wherever possible to greet her or take her picture. Through it all, Patrick did her best to accommodate her fans.

"I think it's very flattering when people look up to you and notice what you're doing," Patrick said. "You do your best to help and accommodate and answer any questions anybody has. It's difficult to act on everything, but you [need to] be there for questions and answers and autographs, and everything they want."[10]

Thanks in large part to the presence of Patrick, the IRL was receiving media coverage like never before. Of course, most of the coverage was about Patrick as she appeared on CNN and ESPN and was on the cover of *Sports Illustrated* and a number of other magazines.

STANDING ON HER OWN

After bursting onto the national scene, Patrick was able to attend a lot of events hosted or attended by athletes from other sports. She got the chance to meet soccer star Mia Hamm and golf stars Annika Sorenstam and Grace Park.

While Patrick is now a role model to millions of young girls, she said she never had role models outside her family while growing up.

Some critics thought she was not deserving of the coverage. She had yet to win a race. Rookies, however, have had trouble winning races in the IRL. Up to that point, Tomas Scheckter was the last rookie to take the checkered flag, winning in 2002 at Michigan. And Patrick was competitive. Through the first twelve races she had five top-ten finishes and had won two poles.

"None of us expected this to happen," Patrick said of her popularity. "Nobody expected it to be so big and so many people interested in it. It makes before seem like I was a nobody compared to what it is now.

"It would be easy for someone to run away with this. If they wanted to think they were hot stuff, it would be easy. I'm aware of the fact that it can go away as easily as it came, and there's a new hot star in town."[11]

While some of her fellow drivers were a little resentful of all of the attention Patrick was getting, many started to understand that while Patrick may be in the spotlight, more attention was being paid to the rest of the drivers as well. Patrick was pleased to see how the rest of her competitors handled the situation.

"I'm flattered that they embrace it all because, gosh, I don't know how I would have taken all those questions about somebody else," she said. "It's a position I haven't really been in. I think they all handled it beautifully. I thank them all for that."[12]

In reality, Patrick performed well despite the circus atmosphere going on around her. She was the IRL's top rookie and raced well in most of her races.

2005 SEASON SUMMARY

Starts	Wins	Top 5	Top 10	Poles	Laps Led
17	0	2	7	3	63

BREAKING INTO
THE MEN'S CLUB

Patrick is the first person to acknowledge that she receives so much attention because she is a woman. She even uses that fact to her advantage, from posing in magazines to selling products geared for women.

Being a woman, however, has also left her open to unfair criticism or complaints. Often, she has to overcome views that are antiquated, at best.

"I've always understood the way it is," she said. "There are so many opportunities I get as a female. Then again, I'm held to a different standard. There's a flip side to everything. It's just the price I have to pay."[1]

While in England, Patrick had to deal with people shunning her because she is a woman. She was dealing mostly with fellow teenagers, however, and believed the way she was treated would change as she grew up and was around other mature people.

That, however, has not always been the case. In May 2005, former open-wheel driver Robby Gordon, who now competes in NASCAR, said Patrick had an unfair advantage against the rest of her competitors because she weighs nearly one hundred pounds less than them.

"The lighter the car, the faster it goes," Gordon said. "Do the math. Put her in the car at her weight, then put me or Tony Stewart in the car at 200 pounds [90.7 kilograms] and our car is at least 100 pounds [43.3 kilograms] heavier.

"I won't race against her until the IRL does something to take that advantage away. Right off the bat, a guy my size is spotting her 105

DID YOU KNOW?

For years Patrick didn't worry too much about what she ate. But because of her grueling job, she pays attention to what she consumes. Her favorite foods are fish, vegetables, and fruit, and she loves to drink water.

pounds [47.6 kilograms]. That's the reason she's so much faster."[2]

In the IRL, the car has to weigh at least 1,525 pounds (691.7 kilograms) before the fuel and driver are added. Some teams in Indy feel Patrick will gain close to one mile per hour in speed because of her small stature. Instead of acknowledging Patrick as a talented driver, comments such as the one Gordon made dismiss her ability.

Gordon later tried to clarify his comment, saying, "I have a problem with the rule, not any particular driver. I've been impressed with Danica from the first time she got in an IRL car earlier this year, and I certainly did not mean to disrespect her or any other driver."[3]

Gordon's comment, however, doesn't compare to some of the other views people have about Patrick. In 2005, Jenson Button, a Formula One driver in Europe, said women such as Patrick are unsafe to drive at a certain time of the month and that their figures would prevent them from being comfortable in a car. He also said mechanics would be distracted by having to deal with a female driver.

Patrick has tried to remain above the remarks about her. She doesn't excuse a loss to a driver because he was stronger and therefore able to drive the car faster.

IT'S THE DRIVER, NOT THE CAR

If comments aren't made about Patrick having a weight advantage or her figure, then some are made about her doing well only because she has good equipment to race with.

Perhaps if the women who came before her had the same type of racing equipment, some critics say, those female drivers would have been more successful than they were. Rahal hates when he hears such comments.

DID YOU KNOW?

Patrick's first dog was named Spike. A miniature schnauzer, Spike used to stand guard next to Patrick's crib.

"I really take offense at that," he said. "She wouldn't have this team behind her if she hadn't earned it. There's a lot of sour grapes out there. [People say] 'Well, she's on this great team, and that's somehow covering up for her deficiencies.' She's here because she deserved a chance to be with a good team."[4]

THE KING WEIGHS IN

Because Button hails from Europe, people may just dismiss his comments about Patrick and female drivers. However, former U.S. race car drivers such as Richard Petty also have problems with female drivers.

Patrick gets in a practice run prior to the 2005 Indianapolis 500.

Petty wasn't thrilled when Janet Guthrie became the first female driver to compete in the Coca-Cola 600 in 1976. After thirty years, his view toward female drivers hasn't changed much.

"I just don't think it's a sport for women," Petty said. "And so far, it's proved out. It's really not. It's good for them to come in. It gives us a lot of publicity, it gives them publicity.

"But as far as being a real true racer, making a living out of it, it's kind of tough."[5]

Guthrie remembers the reception she got from Petty, writing in her book, *Janet Guthrie: A Life at Full Throttle*, "When I shook hands with Richard Petty I thought I'd get frostbite. Later, he would be quoted as saying of me: 'She's no lady. If she was she'd be at home. There's a lot of differences in being a lady and being a woman.'"[6]

Petty admits to being impressed with what Guthrie accomplished, especially since she competed during a time when racing didn't try to promote racing to women or minorities very often.

NOT JUST THE DRIVERS

Petty may be a product of a different time, a time when people had different opinions about what women could and could not do. But Patrick still has to deal with such views today, and not just from fellow drivers.

While some male drivers are intolerant of females intruding into their world, the media emphasize the fact that Patrick is a female and not just another driver. Headlines such as "Dishy Dani's Indy Joy" often focus on Patrick's appearance, not her skills.

Those same articles, however, don't describe her male competitors as "bombshells," or "brunette

NOT MUCH OF A CONCERT!
Patrick went to her first concert when she was six. She and her mom went to see Randy Travis. According to Patrick, she fell asleep and never heard a note.

Janet Guthrie —
Fastest Woman
Behind a Wheel

"Being a Woman Irrelevant on Track" — Janet Guthrie

Racing pioneer Janet Guthrie was the first woman to compete in both the Indy 500 and Daytona 500.

beauties." Instead, the author writes about the skills and abilities of males on the track. Patrick's talent is eventually written about, but usually after her looks are described.

"When people talk about how we look," said former tennis great Billie Jean King, who has been waging the battle against sexism for more than a quarter of a century, "that's what kills us as athletes. Just once, talk only about our accomplishments. That's all we ask."[7]

7

TRAGEDY AND CHANGE

Patrick was full of excitement as the 2006 IRL season approached. She was coming off a successful 2005 campaign in which she earned the Rookie of the Year award. With an additional year of experience, Patrick was positive that 2006 would be a breakout year.

Instead, Patrick had to deal with tragedy, a host of rumors about her future, and inconsistency on the track.

During a warmup session before the season-opening race at

Homestead-Miami Speedway, driver Paul Dana died after sustaining injuries during a crash. Instead of getting ready for the new season, Patrick instead was grieving at a memorial service for a new teammate she barely got to know.

Dana's death made Patrick think about her career and the danger she puts herself into every time she takes her car around the track.

"My husband said it best," said Patrick. "He told me, 'Just because you're a race car driver doesn't mean you're supposed to die.' I think that's the truth of it.

"We've all been doing this a very long time. I'm in my 15th year [in racing] and I'm only 24. A lot of people have a lot of experience out there. We don't really know any different. . . . Everybody knows that we're sort of tempting it with what we do. But I will say that everything that can be done to make the cars safer is being done."[1]

The misfortune of Dana's accident also put Rahal Letterman drivers Patrick and Buddy Rice in a hole to start the season. Co-owners Bobby Rahal and David Letterman withdrew the cars of Patrick and Rice, forcing them to sit out the season-opening race.

The street course in St. Petersburg was the second race of the season, and Patrick was more than ready to start racing again. However, qualifying did not go as well as she hoped, a trend that would continue throughout the season. She had the fourteenth-best time, forcing her to work through a lot of traffic if she wanted to win.

Patrick did all she could to pull out a victory. She deftly steered her car through the congestion on the road. But she couldn't pull off the victory, settling for sixth instead. It was then off to Japan, where she experienced so much success in 2005 with a fourth-place finish after starting second.

But whatever magic she had there in 2005 was gone in 2006. She qualified fourteenth for the second week in a row and finished the race in eighth place. Then came the Indy 500, and once again Patrick was the center of attention. But as was the case in Japan, she was unable to duplicate her success of 2005 at the famed track.

Her qualifying run forced her to start in the tenth position, and she was able to improve by only two spots during the race as she finished eighth. The next week at Watkins Glen produced another eighth-place finish. The good news for Patrick was she had four straight top-ten finishes. The bad news was the fact that her

DID YOU KNOW?

Patrick is in a business in which everything has to be done quickly. But one of her biggest weaknesses is the inclination to procrastinate.

Patrick gets in her car during the time trials for the ABC Supply/AJ Foyt 225 in West Allis, Wisconsin.

qualifying runs were forcing her to start deep in the field.

Patrick and her car were struggling against the top cars in the field, especially those owned by Roger Penske or Chip Ganassi, and frustration was starting to build. Her best starting position in 2006 was tenth, accomplished twice.

"I had my best qualifying lap of the day, then the Penske cars go and crush it by three miles per hour [4.8 kph] and make me look silly," Patrick said before her race at Michigan International Speedway in July.[2] Patrick qualified eleventh out of the nineteen-car field.

By the end of the season, Patrick finished ninth in the points standings, an improvement on her 2005 finish. Her eight top-ten finishes were one better than in 2005 and she had two top-five finishes, the same as 2005 despite competing in four fewer races. The biggest difference was in her qualifying runs.

In 2005, she won three poles and started twelve races in the top ten. She never came close to winning a pole in 2006, starting tenth or worse in all thirteen of her events. The lack of wins and poor qualifying runs led some critics to question her ability on the track.

"[2006] was definitely like, 'Go out there and do the best you can, and bring it home [in one piece],'" Patrick said of her season. "We really did not feel like we had a shot at all."[3]

DEALING WITH RUMORS

Making matters tougher on Patrick throughout the 2006 season was the constant barrage of rumors she had to deal with. The rumors centered around where she would drive in 2007—with Rahal Letterman Racing or a new IRL team. Or would she leave IRL altogether by jumping over to NASCAR, which has more exposure and twice as many races during a season compared to the IRL schedule?

Racing fans throughout the season were mesmerized by visions of Patrick possibly joining the likes of Jeff Gordon and Tony Stewart on a NASCAR track. Juan Pablo Montoya had already announced his decision to join NASCAR in 2007 after a successful career as a Formula One driver.

Everyone was wondering—could Patrick be next?

"It's not a lie that I'm interested [in NASCAR]," Patrick said. "It's definitely something that I look at because it's racing. I'm a race car driver. It's what I do. It's so big it's hard to ignore."[4]

NASCAR officials said they would welcome Patrick and drivers were excited about the prospect of seeing Patrick joining the circuit. She would not only add to the tal-

DID YOU KNOW?

Patrick has a simple outlook on life. Her philosophy is "Life is what you make of it."

ented number of drivers, but she would also bring even more attention to a sport that is growing by leaps and bounds.

"That would be another huge one for sure," said veteran NASCAR driver Mark Martin. "I think it would be great, absolutely fantastic. She is definitely a major, major, major draw."[5]

Adding fuel to the fire was the fact that Patrick's parents, Bev and T. J., were guests of Roush Racing for a NASCAR Nextel Cup race at Chicagoland Speedway one weekend. Patrick was asked questions about her future, especially since her contract with Rahal Letterman was up at the end of the season.

"Contract time is always interesting, and I'm lucky enough you guys pay attention to what I do," Patrick said. "What I'm doing is figuring out what I'm up to for the next couple years of my life. Every decision I make is going to be based on who can get me a car that wins."[6]

DECISION IS FINALLY MADE

The last thing the IRL wanted to see was Patrick jumping to NASCAR. The series struggles enough to get fans to attend races or watch them on television. Rumors are always circulating that teams may jump to the rival Champ Car World Series circuit. Losing Patrick, the IRL's top draw, would be devastating.

As it turned out, the talk about moving to NASCAR was just that—talk. While such a move may still be in Patrick's future, that future was not 2007.

"My heart and soul is in IndyCar racing," Patrick said. "NASCAR is not out for good; it's out for right now."[7]

However, Patrick did announce she was making a change. Starting in 2007, she would be racing for Andretti Green Racing, leaving behind the Rahal Letterman team. Co-owned by longtime driver Michael Andretti, Kim Green, and Kevin Savoree, AGR, at the time of Patrick's signing, claimed twenty-three wins and two titles since joining the series in 2003.

"Andretti Green has won more races than anyone in the series," Patrick said. "I've said all along that my passion, my heart, my soul has always been in IndyCar Racing. If there was a team that was going to give me a chance to win in

DID YOU KNOW?

Patrick doesn't have a lot of time to watch television, but when she does, she said her favorite shows are *Sex and the City*, anything on the Food Network, and the *Late Show with David Letterman*. She does not like to watch westerns or anything that is filmed in black and white.

AN INNER PEACE

In 2004, Patrick made a change in her life, and it started while she was sitting at a coffee shop in Long Beach, California. While looking across the street, she saw a movie theater that was showing *The Passion of the Christ*.

She remembers calling her then-fiancé Paul Hospenthal and asking what his religion was. She learned he was Catholic.

"I was nothing, really, but I always had this sort of faith in the bottom of my heart that I didn't know where it came from," she said. "I had never (gone) to church; we were always racing on Sundays. I just became intrigued.

"I started asking him questions. We talked a lot about it."[8]

One year later, Patrick formally professed her faith, adding to what was already a huge year as she competed in her first Indy 500, embraced Catholicism, and got married.

"It helps me justify situations, that there's a reason for everything," she said of her religion. "It makes me feel better in times when I might have been disappointed or angry."[9]

the Indy Racing League, that's where I'm going to be."[10]

Patrick said the move from Rahal Letterman to AGR was not an easy decision for her to make. It was Rahal who gave her a chance to break into open-wheel racing in the United States. But in the end, the chance to win is what persuaded her to leave Rahal Letterman.

"I've had a very good run, a very good relationship with Rahal Letterman and Bobby Rahal," she said. "He helped me when no one else stepped up, and I will be forever grateful for that.

"But at some point, there's just time for a change, time for something new. I feel Andretti Green is going to give me the opportunity to win races, and while Rahal Letterman still can, too, I have to go with what I think is best for my future. I feel like [Andretti Green] is the place."[11]

Andretti was ecstatic to have Patrick become the newest member of his team. AGR already had one young up-and-coming driver in Marco Andretti, Michael's son. Patrick gave the team two rising superstars.

"Our focus has been and always will be on winning races and winning championships. We certainly believe Danica will do that," he said. "She has made it very clear that one of her goals as a driver is to win the Indianapolis 500 and we are looking forward to giving her a great opportunity to do that."[12]

PRESSURE TO WIN INCREASES

Patrick has always stated that her only real goal in racing is to win. That desire was a main factor in her decision to jump from the Rahal Letterman team to Andretti Green Racing. AGR has been one of the best teams in the IRL since coming aboard in 2003.

"My decision came solely based on where I think I can win," Patrick said about joining AGR. "For me, I believe when I win, everything will take care of itself, so there will be plenty of opportunities, plenty of money, that sort of thing.

"So for me, it's just about winning. It really is . . . what I have to do as a driver to take that next step."[1]

Patrick has accomplished nearly everything else, from being on magazine covers to endorsing a host of products. In 2005, she sold more racing merchandise than all of the other IRL drivers combined.

But during her first two years in the IRL, she did not win a single race. Conversations about Patrick were focusing on her lack of victories. Until she was able to win a race, there would be lingering questions about how good she really was on the track.

"People have said that for a long time," Patrick said. "I can't say I feel a ton of pressure. I feel more. As the years go on, you just hope it happens and you can get it over with.

"But the pressure's healthy. You should be pushed. You should feel like you have to win. If you're out there without pressure, I don't think you get the most out of yourself."[2]

Tony Kanaan, a teammate of Patrick with AGR, said the pressure Patrick is experiencing to win comes with being such a popular driver.

"To be big, you have to take big hits," Kanaan said. "When you're big, you fall bigger than everybody else, too. Everybody has created big expectations for her, but this is racing. How many people want Dale Earnhardt Jr. to win a championship? It hasn't happened yet. I use that example because I'm a fan of Dale."[3]

MONEY, MARKETING ADDING TO PRESSURE?

Patrick has always stated that the chance to earn more money was not the reason for the move to AGR. But changing teams didn't hurt her financially, and former teammate Dan Wheldon says money may be placing even more pressure on Patrick to win.

"Obviously, she's been paid a lot of money to go there," said Wheldon, who left AGR after winning the 2005 title to join Chip Ganassi Racing. "So as the highest paid driver, she should be the one leading the team, right? Is that not correct?"[4]

Patrick wanted to win a race badly. Fans dearly wanted to see her win as well. Advertising executives also yearned for Patrick to start winning races. They worried that she would lose her popularity and be less influential if she did not start winning.

SHE SAID IT
"The good news is that when the race starts, I don't think about that. I don't have time to think about that."

— Danica Patrick on the pressure she feels to win

Patrick talks with her Andretti Green Racing teammates prior to 2007 Indy 500 qualifying races.

Her appeal "could be relatively short-lived because it could be perceived as too gimmicky," says David Carter, executive director of the University of Southern California's Sports Business Institute. "Plenty of athletes have come and gone that were packaged well but didn't win and people tired of them over time."[5]

Patrick is not the only IRL driver to never finish a race in the winner's circle. Two other women drivers in the IRL, Sarah Fisher and Milka Duno, had yet to claim the checkered flag through the 2008 season.

But the pressure to win continued to increase. Teammate Marco Andretti earned his first win in only his thirteenth start. And after placing fourth at the Indy 500 in 2005, Patrick went twenty races before finishing in the top five again. The streak ended when she placed fourth in Nashville in July 2006.

"I do feel more pressure this year," she said about the 2007 season. "But I know it's a matter of time, a matter of everything falling into place at the right time. Unfortunately, the first year I had a fast car but not much experience. And last year I had more experience, but the car was bad. It will come."[6]

Said Michael Andretti: "[The pressure is] not just what she's feeling from the outside. It's more what she's feeling in herself. Because she knows she can do it. She needs to have the day go right for her. If it does, she can do it. We wouldn't have hired her if we didn't think she could win races."[7]

Patrick, her teammates, and her bosses all expected her to eventually win a race. Her competitors, however, also believed it was only a matter of time before she experienced victory.

Jaques Lazier once had a postcrash shouting match with Patrick. He even admits he would like to receive the attention Patrick gets. He also knows that Patrick is a talented and skilled driver who deserves her place in the IRL.

"People always say, 'Why is she still here?' because she hasn't won," says Lazier. "Well, it's because it's so competitive. That team is so good anyone can jump in and do well. She's just been unlucky, and racing takes a lot of luck. I don't think you can question her ability."[8]

A VICTORY TO ENSURE HER ARRIVAL

Bad luck or not, some critics started to compare Patrick to Anna Kournikova, an attractive tennis player who became popular more for her good looks than her talent. While Kournikova reached the finals of four WTA tournaments, she retired without ever winning a singles title.

Similarities between Patrick and Kournikova, fair or unfair, began to grow.

"I see the parallels," Patrick said. "But you know what? It's surface stuff. For one, I'm competing against guys so right off the bat it's different.

"I'm not so worried about that first win. I want it to come, I want it to be over with, but I've been racing up front every weekend and that's a big relief for me because the wins will come. Hey and let's not forget she [Kournikova] was pretty darn good too."[9]

DID YOU KNOW?

Aside from appearing on numerous magazine covers, Patrick has appeared in music videos and in a Super Bowl commercial.

Patrick has brought some of the criticism on herself. In April 2003, she posed for pictures in *FHM* magazine. In several of the pictures, she was baring more skin than clothes. But Patrick refuses to apologize for the photo spread. She did it at a time when she needed a boost in her career, and if using her looks was a way to do so, then that is what she had to do. By 2008, Patrick had turned to bathing suit modeling in the *Sports Illustrated* Swimsuit Edition, which reaches more than 60 million readers worldwide.

Guthrie says finding sponsorship remains extremely difficult for women in racing.

"Danica's appearance in that girlie magazine established a persona that a number of women drivers weren't happy to see but was very clearly successful for her," Guthrie says. "You might call it old-fashioned, but most of us wanted to be judged on the basis of what we accomplished [instead of] how we looked. I'm sure she does, too, but she's not been reluctant to take advantage of her marketable good looks."[10]

St. James, who has known Patrick since she was thirteen, said there is a double standard when it comes to women and men and marketing. Why should Patrick posing in a magazine raise controversy but NASCAR driver Carl Edwards posing bare-chested on an *ESPN The Magazine* cover doesn't?

Michael Andretti, in black shirt, stepped away from the driver's seat in 2007 in order to focus on ownership.

"Some guys have an extra advantage because of their looks, and other guys that aren't so good looking still get sponsors and get to race," says St. James. "But for women, you're judged on performance, but you have an extra scale of how you look because women are always judged that way because of society."[11]

WINNING CURES A LOT

Patrick knew the easiest way to turn the discussion of her career back to racing was to win. One victory would quiet a lot of the critics. "What I always kept in mind, and what I really believe, I just need to win," she said. "Wherever I'm at, it will be a big deal when I win,

and a lot of other things will materialize and things will happen."[12]

9

ROLE MODEL AND MORE

Patrick is not the first female to shine in the athletic arena. Maria Sharapova (tennis), Lorena Ochoa (golf), and Lisa Leslie (basketball) are all superstars in their respective sports. But unlike those three athletes, Patrick has had to overcome a gender barrier to succeed.

Leslie has had to compete only against fellow female basketball players. Sharapova and Ochoa only compete against other women. Patrick, however, competes in a sport dominated by men.

"She is a great role model," said Brooke deLench, the executive director of Momsteam.com, a support Web site for parents. "She has faced some opposition, but she has been able to stand right up to them. It's typically a male sport, but frankly, women are great drivers."[1]

Patrick was thrust into the spotlight in 2005 after her performance in the Indy 500. Before the race, only true fans of racing knew of her. After the Indy 500, seemingly everyone in the United States became familiar with Patrick, thanks in large part to *Sports Illustrated* putting her on the cover of the magazine after she led the Indy 500.

Suddenly, Patrick was known everywhere. She had a whole new legion of fans, many of them young females who were barely younger than Patrick, who was only twenty-three when she joined the IRL. Not surprisingly, Patrick was caught a little off guard by the sudden fame.

"It's something that really hit me in Indianapolis, especially with all of the mail [from fans]," she said. "I'm not actively trying to be a role model. It's something I didn't think was going to come so soon.

"If I'm going to be a role model, I think that the message needs to be as simple as: do it because you love it. Do it because it's what you want to . . . not because your role model does it."[2]

Perhaps not in tune to just how popular she was after the Indy 500, Patrick believed the attention surrounding her would be over fairly quickly.

"All I knew was the best-case scenario it would be big news and it would help the series and inspire young kids and girls and be a really great story," she said of her Indi-anapolis 500 record-setting debut. "It's a big deal, but I don't think it's something I'm going to over-analyze and say, 'Wow, I'm in the newspapers every day and I made *Us Weekly*.'"[3]

DID YOU KNOW?

Before becoming a race car driver, Patrick's first job was working for her parents at the Oil Exchange in Roscoe, Illinois, as a cashier. She later worked for her parents at the Java Hut.

CALM AND COOL

Patrick's actions are just as important as her words in her position as a role model. She has often been the target of subtle abuse from fellow male competitors. The abuse came in the form of words, or lack of them, as many fellow competitors didn't want to talk to her during her time in England.

When words were spoken, they were often condescending and demeaning. Bernie Ecclestone of Formula One once said, "Women should be all dressed in white like other domestic appliances." The comment came during questions about Patrick following her Indy 500 debut.

But instead of replying in kind to Ecclestone, Patrick shrugged off the comment.

"What I like about her is she is at the top of her game," said Carrie Lukas, the vice president of policy at the Independent Women's Forum. "No one is doing her any favors or changing the rules so she can compete against men. It's frustrating because you can't escape the fact that beauty plays a role. It's the reality of sports as a business, but she handles it well and doesn't play any victim role."[4]

For her part, Patrick tries to downplay being a role model. She wants to help her sport succeed, through higher ratings, better attendance, or through improved racing on the track. But she doesn't feel she has to perform better just because she garners a lot of attention.

DID YOU KNOW?

It didn't take long for Patrick to get her first speeding ticket. Not long after getting her Mustang Cobra, Patrick was pulled over for going 65 miles per hour (105 kph) in a 45 miles per hour (72 kph) zone. Patrick's excuse was that she was just using her new car's potential.

"I have a problem with people thinking that because there's exposure, that I have to do something," she said. "I don't feel like I have to do anything. I feel I have to get the most out of myself, but that's it. I'm living up to myself, and that's all I can do."[5]

Patrick says she didn't have any role models as a child, except for her parents. She wanted a career in auto racing because that is what she wanted to do, not because that is what someone else had already done.

"I didn't have athletes or celebrities or anybody in particular that I looked to throughout my whole career," Patrick said. "There were people along the way that I felt like I learned from. But I learned from them because I was standing next to them.

"I've never gauged myself off of other women. Maybe that's what has gotten me to where I am. My interest is in being the fastest and the best, not the fastest girl or the best girl."[6]

Despite all the attention that stardom has brought, Patrick says her personality has not changed.

While she may not be completely comfortable with the expectations placed on her, Patrick has done her best to set an example for fans and to remain true to herself. But she has embraced her position and if she says something or does something to inspire another person, she is happy.

"I didn't think I'd be so much of a role model as I was or as I am. But I think that, as I've said before, the best part about all that is I've never changed who

I am. I've never tried to be a role model," Patrick said. "I guess I've never tried to act a part and say the right things or do the right things. I just think that I was brought up with good values and have good parents that were good role models for me when I was growing up."[7]

GIVING BACK TO OTHERS

Patrick has always been close to her family. Her parents have always been there to support her and her racing career. Without the support of Bev and T. J., Patrick might not even be racing today.

But Patrick also knows how fortunate she has been to have that support. There are a lot of people who are alone or are facing tough circumstances, sometimes with the support of family and friends and other times with no support at all.

Patrick saw an opportunity to help one of her favorite charities, Best Buddies Indiana, which helps people overcome intellectual disabilities. During the Indy 500 in 2005, she damaged the wing to the No. 16 Rahal Letterman Racing car she was driving.

The section costs approximately $5,000. But with the national frenzy associated with Patrick, it quickly became apparent that the wing could be auctioned and the money raised go to Best Buddies Indiana. Panther Racing, with the blessing of Rahal

Letterman Racing, had Patrick sign the wing and placed it on eBay. The surprise was the amount the wing sold for. J. B. Moresco put in a winning bid of $42,650.01 to purchase the wing.

Whenever possible, Patrick attends charity events or visits children's hospitals. While in Nashville for the Firestone Indy 200 in 2005, Patrick was invited to visit with patients at the Monroe Carell Jr. Children's Hospital at Vanderbilt. Joe M. Dorris, a personal sponsor of Patrick and president of the Futaba Corporation of America, extended the invitation to Patrick. Dorris said he wanted the young patients to meet Patrick, who he says has the natural air of a professional to match her skill behind the wheel.

Patrick, who was accompanied by hospital Child Life staff, went from one room to another to visit with patients. She signed hats and cards for the children and their family members as well.

"For someone who is so young and who has gained national attention in such a short period of time, Danica is impressive," Dorris said. "She didn't

SHE SAID IT
"I doubt I'll be racing [in 15 years]. I'll evolve and grow into another spot. I'm sure it'll be linked [to racing] because that's my identity."

— Danica Patrick

want this visit to be about her, she had a genuine desire to do something nice for the children."[8]

"If I can be a role model for young people, that's great," Patrick said during her visit. "And this is a great place to be able to serve in that role."[9]

JUST A RACE CAR DRIVER

Patrick has accepted her role as a role model. She enjoys bringing a smile to a young, ill child's face. She is thrilled to be an inspiration to young girls, proving that they can succeed in any field.

But in the future, whenever she is making a public appearance or raising money for a charity, she hopes to be introduced as one of the IRL's top drivers, not as the best female driver or first female to win the Indy 500. To be a true role model, she believes no title should be attached to her name other than "race car driver."

"My goal is not to be the first female to do things, or it's not to be a poster child or a calendar girl," she said. "It's to just win, because everything else takes care of itself when you win."[10]

For a legion of younger fans, they understand Patrick's desire to shed the "female" label. Many already have looked past the fact that she is a woman. They only see her for what she really is—a race car driver.

BREAKING THROUGH

As the 2007 season approached, Patrick was almost feeling like a rookie again. Yes, she had thirty races under her belt, but she was now with a new team. By joining AGR, she believed she had everything in place to seriously challenge for a win.

Before she could concentrate on winning, however, she had to get to know her new team, from her fellow drivers to the engineers and crew members. "There are more people, different people, different information in different surroundings at the new team," she said.[1]

What didn't take a lot of time was the bonding Patrick and her teammates started to experience. As the new member of the team, she could have easily been left out by teammates Tony Kanaan, Dario Franchitti, and Marco Andretti. Instead, the foursome was often seen together and trading jokes with one another, something that didn't always happen on her old team.

"It's fun. We go out to dinner together," she said. "We have more friendship than I've experienced before. They're fantastic drivers and they are friends. That's something new to me."[2]

While all of the drivers are looking to win, they don't keep information to themselves. Kanaan often speaks with Patrick to offer advice or encouragement.

"I definitely am among a group of drivers that push you to reach the next level because they're so good," Patrick said. "I think all of those things are what's going to really take it all up a notch and hopefully get that first win."[3]

Patrick's boss, Michael Andretti, also offers advice, drawing upon his past experience as a successful driver. "Michael has been helpful giving me advice, outside of the engineer and teammates, and giving me the benefit of his past experience as far as driving," said Patrick. "He's very valuable to me, helping me choose what's best for me out there."[4]

Patrick prepares to head out on the track during qualifying for a race in 2007.

SLOW START

Patrick's enthusiasm for the start of the season didn't carry over and turn into instant success on the track. In the season-opening race at Homestead, she placed fourteenth after qualifying thirteenth.

She did a little better on the road course in St. Petersburg, finishing eighth. Then it was off to Japan, where Patrick has had mixed success. The weekend started well for her as she had the fourth-best qualifying run. But she was unable to keep the momentum going during the race as she struggled for much of the day and finished eleventh.

The fourth race of the season was at the Kansas Speedway. Qualifying did not go as well as Patrick wished, as she placed tenth. However, she improved on that showing during the race and finished seventh, her best showing of the young season.

BACK AT INDY

With the first four races out of the way, the teams could concentrate on the spectacle that is the Indy 500. This is where Patrick burst onto the scene, becoming an overnight sensation after becoming the first woman to lead the race and finishing fourth, the highest finish ever for a female.

The following year, high expectations followed Patrick, though the media crush wasn't as bad as in 2005. Patrick was unable to duplicate her 2005 showing, however, finishing eighth after starting in tenth.

Despite the early ups and downs of the 2007 season, Patrick was showing improvement on the track in each race. She was getting more comfortable with her crew. Mario Andretti said Patrick was a force to be reckoned with. Her boss, Michael Andretti, was confident Patrick could contend for an Indy 500 victory.

"If she can get the car right for herself, she's going to be a real factor on race day," Andretti said.[5]

From 1996–2004, the name "Danica," which is Slavic meaning "morning star," didn't rank in the top 1,000 baby names. But since 2005, when Patrick finished fourth in the Indy 500 and won the Bombardier Learjet Rookie of the Year award, the name "Danica" has been climbing up the charts. It was the 610th-most popular name in 2006 and jumped to 352nd in 2006.

As the 2007 event drew closer, Patrick believed she had learned from her first two races at the famed racetrack and could make a serious run for the checkered flag.

"I've learned what a car is supposed to feel like," Patrick said. "It's given me the ability to demand certain things out of myself and the engineers as far as the way the car handles."[6]

Race day finally came and so, too, did the rain. As the race unfolded between delays, it was evident that Patrick had the talent to run with the best drivers in the field, even though her eighth-place finish suggests otherwise. Her car was not handling well at the start of the race, but she maneuvered through the field to vault into third place before the first storm came. The rain started to fall, forcing a red flag and sending everyone to pit row.

The delay lasted nearly three hours. When racing finally resumed, Patrick zoomed by teammate

Marco Andretti on Lap 120 to take second place. Everything was going well for Patrick except for her inability to pass Kanaan, another teammate. She followed closely behind him for the next seventeen laps.

When the caution flag came out, Patrick and many others in the lead pack pitted to get fresh tires and some fuel. The strategy was smart, but as it turned out, the timing was unlucky.

When Patrick came back onto the track, she was in the back of the pack. The good news was many of the drivers in front of her were on a schedule to pit soon, meaning Patrick would again be near the front of the pack. But the rain came once again and forced the race to eventually end thirty-four laps early. Instead of possibly earning a podium finish, Patrick came in eighth, the same result as 2006.

"We'll win this one, I promise," she said. "We'll win it at some point. I know we will. We had a great shot at it. Darn the rain, huh?"[7]

After the race, Patrick was only disappointed in the fact that the rain played havoc with the race, keeping the drivers from settling the outcome themselves. However, she did show some frustration when comparing this race to her first two and not being able to claim the checkered flag. "[This race was] probably the most frustrating of all just because I really felt like I had a chance," she said. "I had a fast car.

"It's this elusive win that keeps sitting on my shoulder. We had a chance today, just like I thought we did coming into the event. But then again, we all did at AGR, as you could see throughout the race. Someone was always in position to finish first."[8]

THE SEASON GOES ON

The following week at the ABC Supply/A. J. Foyt 225, Patrick finished eighth after qualifying seventeenth. But what happened after the race drew more attention than what occurred on the track.

On Lap 88, Patrick was in fifth place when she bumped Dan Wheldon in Turn 1. Though Wheldon was slightly ahead and on the outside, Patrick wasn't about to give in. Patrick briefly lost control of the car before she saved it.

While Wheldon went on to finish third, Patrick had to scramble back through the field to place eighth. After the race, Patrick confronted Wheldon, grabbed his arm and gave him a shove. Wheldon spoke about the incident afterward. "She's just being Danica," he said. "She'll be fine when she calms down. She's mess-

2007 SEASON SUMMARY

STARTS	WINS	TOP-FIVES	TOP-TENS	POLES	FINISH
17	0	4	11	0	7

ing with the wrong person if she wants to get feisty. I'm a lot tougher than she is on the track."[9]

The next race at Texas Motor Speedway was billed as the "Rumble at the Speedway" by race promoters, playing off what happened between Wheldon and Patrick in Milwaukee. Race fans didn't see any more fireworks between the two drivers. Instead, they saw some great racing and a career-best finish by Patrick.

DID YOU KNOW?

Patrick has taken on the men of the Indy Racing League, and now she wants to compete in the fashion industry. Patrick said she would love to land more endorsement deals for fashion, fragrance, and beauty products. If possible, she would enjoy starting her own clothing line.

The two drivers were driving side-by-side on the fourth lap and stayed close together for the next fourteen laps. But both drivers made sure they gave enough space for them both to race. Wheldon finally pulled away and stayed ahead until being knocked out of the race on Lap 197.

As for Patrick, she avoided the accidents that knocked out several drivers and dashed across the finish line in third place for her best-ever finish at the time.

"Maybe we should make you mad more often," joked Kanaan, her Andretti Green teammate.[10]

DID YOU KNOW?

Patrick was voted the most popular IndyCar driver for the third straight year in 2007. The award is determined by fan voting at every IRL event during the season. Patrick joined Sarah Fisher as the only three-time fan favorites in the IRL's eleven-year history.

Said Patrick: "There's a story, and all of a sudden I have a season-best. It was really just a matter of time I think. We've had fast cars. It's a shame Tony and I didn't have more time to get Sam [Hornish Jr., who won the race]."[11]

Overall, she finished the season seventh, her best finish yet in her three-year IndyCar career.

Throughout the season she proved she belonged on the track. A break here or there and she would have finally earned her first career win. With the 2008 season rapidly approaching, Patrick won't have too much time to reflect on her season.

She didn't earn her first win in 2007, but she proved that a woman can compete with the men.

"I'm a pretty ordinary girl who was blessed with extraordinary purpose and ambition. I'm a small-town girl who had a dream and a family who helped her believe that anything is possible," said Patrick. "I am living proof that if you work hard and aim high, you can do whatever you set your mind to, even if that makes you different. Take it from me; what makes you different makes you great.”[12]

A WIN AT LAST

In 2008, greatness was just around the corner. She was prepared to take another step deeper into stardom. She was in the running in fifteen of the seventeen races in the IndyCar season. In fact, she finished in the top ten in ten of those, only one off her pace of eleven top-ten finishes in 2007.

Her consistency on the track kept her in the top ten of the IndyCar points race throughout the season, with the prospects for improving on her seventh-place finish in 2007 looking brighter. One race, however, shot her to the top of the sporting world.

On April 19, 2008, Patrick won the Indy Japan 300 race at Twin Ring Motegi in Motegi, Japan.

Patrick's trips to Japan had not been horrible leading into the 2008 race at the 1.5-mile (2.5 km) Twin Ring Motegi oval course. In 2005, she qualified second but finished fourth. She started fourteenth in 2006, and finished eighth. By 2007, she started fourth and finished eleventh.

Her fiftieth career start—and her fourth time in the lineup in Japan—would prove to be momentous. When she drove into Victory Lane, she became the first woman to do so in an Indy Car race.

Patrick's victory in Japan was historic on many fronts. In becoming the first woman to win an IndyCar race, Patrick made an impact for women in sports. Later in 2008, the Women's Sports Foundation, in conjunction with the thirty-fifth anniversary of Billie Jean King defeating Bobby Riggs in a man-vs.-woman tennis match, ranked the "35 Most Memorable Moments in Women's Sports" over the last thirty-five years. Patrick's feat was ranked twenty-eighth on the list.

Patrick was in tears after she was overcome with emotion following the race.

"I looked like a chick, like a baby woman!" the 26-year-old Patrick said in an interview with *USA Today* after returning to the United States. "It was pretty bad. . . . I didn't expect to get emotional, but that's what was lying underneath and how much blood, sweat, and tears has gone into getting that first win out of the way.

"I was embarrassed with all the photographers there and took the helmet off to cover my face. Then I said, 'This is how I feel, and this is what sports are all about.'"[13]

Patrick opted not to pit in the last fifty laps of the 200-lap race, and she was only one of three drivers to take that approach. Patrick, who qualified in sixth, passed Helio Castroneves with three laps remaining and held on for the victory.

Patrick holds her trophy after winning the Indy Japan 300 on April 20, 2008.

"With five laps to go, I was saving fuel," Castroneves said. "When Danica passed me, I realized she was the leader. She did a great job, passed me fair and square and that shows you how competitive our series is."[14]

Patrick finished nearly six seconds ahead of Castroneves, who had entered the race in the pole position. Patrick took advantage of a pit stop by leader Scott Dixon with five laps to go. Fellow contenders Dan Wheldon and Tony Kanaan followed with pit stops on the next lap.

"She raced in the top five all day. If anyone tries to say that not all drivers were here or it was a fuel-mileage strategy, they just have a negative attitude about her winning," Indy Racing League president Brian Barnhardt said.[15]

Unfortunately from a marketing and promotional aspect, Patrick's victory in Japan happened when most fans in the United States were already asleep. That it occurred overnight might have lessened its impact on sports fans in the United States.

"Ideally, it happens on U.S. soil between 1–5 p.m. and more people see it, and that might impact their [IRL] ability to capitalize on it to some degree," said Mike Bartelli, president of motor sports for Millsport, a sports marketing consulting group. "But it's

TOP SELLER

Patrick's merchandise outsold that of any other driver, ten to one, according to an IndyCar Series official.

fantastic because it validates her talent and establishes her as a legitimate world-class race car driver."[16]

Patrick figured the victory was just the first of many to come. After securing her first Indy Racing League victory, Patrick was already setting her sights on higher goals.

"Winning was the step I needed to take to move into contending for a championship," she said. "I needed to get over that hurdle. Now I just need to win more."[17]

Michael Andretti, co-owner of AGR, was elated to see his driver come through with her first title.

"I think Danica is such a fantastic person and I'm thrilled for her that the monkey is finally off of her back," Andretti said. "We have all believed in her and she proved today that she is a winner. Frankly, I think this is the first of many."[18]

From making her way to television talk shows to appearing in media with worldwide clout, Patrick thrived in the spotlight.

"I feel way too young to be giving life advice, but this is a great platform to have," Patrick said. "This reaches outside racing. This is about finding something you love to do, and following through with it. . . . It's going to be nice not to have to answer those questions [about winning] anymore. . . . because I believed in myself. I just didn't know when it was going to happen."[19]

With her first title in hand, Patrick was on her way to a career-best finish of sixth place in the Indy Racing League standings.

BACK AT INDY

Returning to the United States, Patrick slipped in her first race after winning a title. She qualified third, but finished nineteenth at Kansas Speedway on April 27, 2008.

Patrick was back in the spotlight over Memorial Day weekend for the Indianapolis 500. This time, she returned to Indianapolis as an IndyCar champion.

After qualifying fifth, the eyes of the sporting world were on Patrick on race day. Already the first woman to win an IndyCar series race, could she win her first Indianapolis 500 title? Patrick wound up with a disappointing twenty-second place after getting knocked out of the race on pit road. Patrick was again part of a media frenzy in Indianapolis when she

2008 SEASON SUMMARY

STARTS	WINS	TOP-FIVES	TOP-TENS	POLES	FINISH
17	1	3	10	0	6

walked down to Ryan Briscoe's pit to confront him after Briscoe's car collided with her car on pit road. Security personnel prevented Patrick from a face-to-face meeting after both drivers had been knocked out of the race.

Sometimes, her temper boils, and she deals with it as only she knows how.

"I wouldn't change anything," Patrick said prior to a race in August 2008. "I'm not a big fan of regret or anything like that. They [emotional outbursts] are not necessarily right or wrong. They just happen."[20]

STAYING IN THE NEWS

Patrick's fiery attitude kept her in the news more than her racing after the Indy 500. She had another confrontation, this time with fellow female driver Milka Duno at Mid-Ohio, where Patrick finished twelfth. Patrick took issue with Duno after Duno cut her off during practice. After some foul language was exchanged between the two drivers and Duno threw a towel at Patrick, the meeting ended.

Although virtually nothing happened, each of Patrick's moves continues to be scrutinized by the media, and is the subject of racing chatter nationwide.

"It's been a year of ups and downs, and drama," Patrick said. "It's either been something on the track drawing attention or something off the track."[21]

After the Indy 500, Patrick finished ninth and tenth in the next two races and was on her way to five top-ten finishes in six races. She had consecutive sixth-place finishes at Iowa Speedway and at Richmond International Raceway. After a fourteenth-place finish at Watkins Glen, Patrick qualified second at Nashville Speedway and finished fifth.

Patrick, however, failed to continue the momentum leading into the latter half of the season. She managed only two top-ten finishes in a string of six races. Her qualifying position of third at Chicagoland Speedway was followed up by a tenth-place finish in the final points race of the season.

TRUE TO HERSELF

With more than $3 million in earnings and a legion of fans following her every move, Patrick has found that being herself is the most effective way to combat any negative situations that arise as one of the most popular female athletes in the world.

"There's absolutely nothing I can do to make everyone happy," Patrick said. "No matter who we are and what we do we're going to make someone mad somewhere. I'm the same. Just on a grander scale, maybe, than some other people."[22]

There's no denying that Patrick stands up for what she believes in. Sometimes her actions don't sit well with others. Other times, she can do no wrong in the eyes of her fans. Regardless of what others think about her, Patrick will likely be in racing's crosshairs for many years to come.

CAREER STATISTICS

Year	Rank	Starts	Wins
2008	6	17	1
2007	7	17	0
2006	9	14	0
2005	12	17	0

Poles	Top 5	Top 10	Points
0	3	10	379
0	4	11	424
0	2	8	302
3	2	7	325

CAREER ACHIEVEMENTS

- In 2008, became first woman to win an IndyCar race.

- Recorded eleven top-ten finishes in 2007, a career high.

- Improved in the points standings in each of her first four seasons on the IndyCar circuit.

- Was the first woman to ever hold a lead in the Indy 500, accomplishing the feat in 2005.

- Finished fourth at the 2005 Indy 500, the best finish ever by a female driver.

- Became the first female driver to win a pole position in the Toyota Atlantic Championship series when she did so in 2004 in Round 5 at Portland.

- **Finished third in the Toyota Atlantic Championship standings in 2004 with 269 points.**

- **Became the first female to earn a podium result in the thirty-year history of the Toyota Atlantic Championship with a third-place finish at Monterrey, Mexico, in 2003.**

- **Won the Gorsline Scholarship Award for top upcoming road racing driver in 2001.**

- **Finished second in the Formula Ford Festival in England in 2000, equaling the highest-ever finish by an American.**

- **Named Bombardier Rookie of the Year in 2005.**

CHAPTER NOTES

CHAPTER 1. BURSTING ONTO THE SCENE

1. Mark Alesia, "Patrick shows she belongs with strong run at Indy," The Indianapolis Star, May 29, 2005, <http://www.usatoday.com/sports/motor/irl/indy500/2005-05-29-patrick_x.htm> (September 8, 2007).

2. Ibid.

3. Alesia, May 29, 2005.

4. Gary Graves, "Patrick looks ahead; Wheldon comes through for Andretti," USA Today, May 31, 2005, <http://www.usatoday.com/sports/motor/irl/indy500/2005-05-30-patrick-wheldon_x.htm> (September 8, 2007).

5. Steve Herman, "Rookie driver races to impressive time," Deseret News (Salt Lake City), May 5, 2005, <http://findarticles.com/p/articles/mi_qn4188/is_20050509/ai_n14619681> (September 8, 2007).

6. Herb Gould, "Girl Vision," Chicago Sun-Times, May 29, 2005, <http://findarticles.com/p/articles/mi_qn4155/is_20050529/ai_n14662843> (September 8, 2007).

7. Ibid.

8. Herman, May 5, 2005.

9. Gould, May 29, 2005.

10. Graves, May 31, 2005.

CHAPTER 2. GROWING UP IN ILLINOIS

1. Andrew Seligman, "Danica backed by folks at home," Deseret News (Salt Lake City), May 29, 2005, <http://findarticles.com/p/articles/mi_qn4188/is_20050529/ai_n14647013> (September 8, 2007).

2. Ibid.

3. Lisa Young Stiers, "Danica Patrick Races into Town for Her Third Running in the Indianapolis 500," Indy's Child, May 1, 2007, <http://www.indyschild.com/1editorialbody.lasso?-token.folder=2007-05-01&-token.story-191981.112112&token.subpub> (September 9, 2007).

4. Tom Weir, "Danica plans to deliver at Indy," USA Today, May 23, 2005, <http://www.usatoday.com/sports/motor/irl/indy500/2005-05-23-cover-patrick_x.htm> (September 9, 2007).

5. Stiers, May 1, 2007.

6. Herb Gould, "Girl Vision," Chicago Sun-Times, May 29, 2005, <http://findarticles.com/p/articles/mi_qn4155/is_20050529/ai_n14662843> (September 8, 2007).

7. Weir, May 23, 2005.

8. Brian Gomez, "All Eyes on Danica," The Gazette (Colorado Springs), Aug. 17, 2005, <http://findarticles.com/p/articles/mi_qn4191/is_20050817/ai_n14918768/pg_1> (September 10, 2007).

9. Stiers, May 1, 2007.

10. Weir, May 23, 2005.

11. "Danica Patrick, race car driver," Current Biography, October, 2005, <http://www.hwwilson.com/Currentbio/cover_bios/cover_bio_10_05.htm> (September 8, 2007).

CHAPTER 3. APPRENTICESHIP IN ENGLAND

1. "Danica Patrick seeks path to the top in 2002," Autoracing1.com, April, 2002, <http://www.autoracing1.com/htmfiles/2002/CART/0401DanicaPR.htm> (September 9, 2007).

2. Ibid.

3. Ibid.

4. Tom Weir, "Danica plans to deliver at Indy," USA Today, May 23, 2005, <http://www.usatoday.com/sports/motor/irl/indy500/2005-05-23-cover-patrick_x.htm> (September 9, 2007).

5. Ibid.

6. "Danica's come a long way on the track, in life," Associated Press, May 27, 2006, <http://www.msnbc.msn.com/id/12997252/> (September 9, 2007).

7. Herb Gould, "Girl Vision," Chicago Sun-Times, May 29, 2005, <http://findarticles.com/p/articles/mi_qn4155/is_20050529/ai_n14662843> (September 8, 2007).

8. "Danica Patrick seeks path to the top in 2002," Autoracing1.com, April, 2002, <http://www.autoracing1.com/htmfiles/2002/CART/0401DanicaPR.htm> (September 9, 2007).

9. Ibid.

10. Weir, May 23, 2005.

11. Dan Carney, "Profile: Danica Patrick," Europeancarweb.com, 2002, <http://www.europeancarweb.com/features/0306ec_danica_patrick/index.html> (September 10, 2007).

12. Ibid.

13. "Danica Patrick, race car driver," Current Biography, October, 2005, <http://www.hwwilson.com/Currentbio/cover_bios/cover_bio_10_05.htm> (September 8, 2007).

CHAPTER 4. BACK TO THE USA

1. Lisa Young Stiers, "Danica Patrick Races into Town for Her Third Running in the Indianapolis 500," Indy's Child, May 1, 2007, <http://www.indyschild.com/1editorialbody.lasso?-token.folder=2007-05-01&-token.story-191981.112112&token.subpub> (September 9, 2007).

2. Ibid.

3. Robin Miller, "Danica Patrick has the ability, and now, the opportunity," Speedtv.com, December 8, 2004, <http://www.speedtv.com/commentary/14283/> (September 11, 2007).

4. "Danica's come a long way on the track, in life," Associated Press, May 27, 2006, <http://www.msnbc.msn.com/id/12997252/> (September 9, 2007).

5. Miller, December 8, 2004.

6. Ibid.

7. Ibid.

8. "Danica Patrick: Danica Patrick logs first day on track in Barber Dodge Pro Series, Racerchicks.com, July 5, 2002, <http://www.racerchicks.com/racers/patrick.html> (September 9, 2007).

9. "Danica Patrick, race car driver," Current Biography, October, 2005," <http://www.hwwilson.com/Currentbio/cover_bios/cover_bio_10_05.htm> (September 8, 2007).

10. Ibid.

CHAPTER 5. ROOKIE OF THE YEAR

1. Anne Proffit, "Danica's come a long way on the track, in life," Motorsports.com, March 1, 2005," <http://www.motorsport.com/news/article.asp?ID=178277>(September 9, 2007).

2. Ibid.

3. Ibid.

4. "Patrick resting after Miami accident," Indycar.com, March 9, 2005, <http://www.indycar.com/news/story.php?story_id=4165> (September 23, 2007).

5. Curt Cavin, "Life takes a sharp turn for Patrick," The Indianapolis Star, May 12, 2006, <http://marriage.about.com/gi/dynamic/offsite.htm?zi=1/XJ&sdn=marriage&cdn=people&tm=270&gps=94_2248_796_445&f=10&tt=11&bt=0&bts=0&zu=http%3A//www.azcentral.com/sports/speed/articles/0512danica0512.html>(September 8, 2007).

6. Ibid.

7. Ibid.

8. Dave Lewandowski, "Toyota, Honda share front row," Indycar.com, April 29, 2005, <http://www.indycar.com/news/story.php?story_id=4436> (September 23, 2007).

9. Dave Lewandowski, "Fireworks in the Heartland," Indycar.com, July 3, 2005, <http://www.indycar.com/news/story.php?story_id=4980> (September 23, 2007).

10. Brian Gomez, "All Eyes on Danica," *The Gazette* (Colorado Springs), Aug. 17, 2005, <http://findarticles.com/p/articles/mi_qn4191/is_20050817/ai_n14918768/pg_1> (September 10, 2007).

11. Ibid.

12. "An interview with Danica Patrick, Geoff Dodge, Jeff Boerger and Ed Van Petten," March 14, 2006, <http://www.indycar.com/news/story.php?story_id=6104> (September 23, 2007).

CHAPTER 6. BREAKING INTO THE MEN'S CLUB

1. "Danica's come a long way on the track, in life," Associated Press, May 27, 2006, <http://www.msnbc.msn.com/id/12997252/> (September 9, 2007).

2. "Robby Gordon raining on Danica's parade," ESPN.com, May 28, 2005, <http://sports.espn.go.com/rpm/news/story?series=wc&id=2070899> (September 9, 2007).

3. Jenna Fryer, "R. Gordon meant no disrespect of Patrick in weight remarks," USA Today, May 31, 2005, <http://www.usatoday.com/sports/motor/irl/indy500/2005-05-31-gordon-patrick_x.htm> (September 12, 2007).

4. Herb Gould, "Girl Vision," Chicago Sun-Times, May 29, 2005, <http://findarticles.com/p/articles/mi_qn4155/is_20050529/ai_n14662843> (September 8, 2007).

5. "Petty hasn't changed views on women racers," ESPN.com, June 1.2006, <http://sports.espn.go.com/espn/wire?section=auto&id=2458321> (September 9, 2007).

6. Ibid.

7. Ian O'Connor, "Wheels of progress turn slowly for women," USA Today, May 31, 2007, <http://www.usatoday.com/sports/columnist/oconnor/2005-05-30-oconnor_x.htm> (September 18, 2007).

CHAPTER 7. TRAGEDY AND CHANGE

1. Mike Harris, "After tragedy, Patrick back in gear," Chicago Sun-Times, April 2, 2006, <http://findarticles.com/p/articles/mi_qn4155/is_20060402/ai_n16207124> (September 8, 2007).

2. Larry Lage, "Danica may be headed for NASCAR," Deseret News (Salt Lake City), July 30, 2006, <http://findarticles.com/p/articles/mi_qn4188/is_20060730/ai_n16648052> (September 8, 2007).

3. Ed Hinton, "Acting Has Vanished for Danica Patrick," The Orlando Sentinel, May 24, 2007, <http://www.theledger.com/apps/pbcs.dll/article?AID=/20070524/NEWS/705240548/0/FRONTPAGE> (September 8, 2007).

4. Teresa M. Walker, "Danica admits NASCAR interest," Chicago Sun-Times, July 14, 2006, <http://findarticles.com/p/articles/mi_qn4155/is_20060714/ai_n16544701> (September 8, 2007).

5. Michael Marot, "Danica may be headed for NASCAR," Deseret News (Salt Lake City), July 11, 2006, <http://findarticles.com/p/articles/mi_qn4188/is_20060711/ai_n16527271> (September 8, 2007).

6. Walker, July 14, 2006.

7. Hunter Atkins, "Patrick to stay in IRL, move to Andretti Green in '07," Chicago Sun-Times, July 16, 2006, <http://findarticles.com/p/articles/mi_qn4155/is_20060726/ai_n16637659> (September 8, 2007).

8. Curt Cavin, "Life takes a sharp turn for Patrick," The Indianapolis Star, May 12, 2006, <http://marriage.about.com/gi/dynamic/offsite.htm?zi=1/XJ&sdn=marriage&cdn=people&tm=270&gps=94_2248_796_445&f=10&tt=11&bt=0&bts=0&zu=http%3A//www.azcentral.com/sports/speed/articles/0512danica0512.html> (September 8, 2007).

9. Ibid.

10. "IRL relieved that Danica's staying," Deseret News (Salt Lake City), July 26, 2006, <http://findarticles.com/p/articles/mi_qn4188/is_20060726/ai_n16636176> (September 8, 2007).

11. Atkins, July 16, 2006.

12. "IRL relieved that Danica's staying," Deseret News (Salt Lake City), July 26, 2006, <http://findarticles.com/p/articles/mi_qn4188/is_20060726/ai_n16636176> (September 8, 2007).

CHAPTER 8. PRESSURE TO WIN INCREASES

1. Jack Rux, "Danica just wants to win, baby Patrick: Switching teams was not," Oakland Tribune, August 25, 2006, <http://findarticles.com/p/articles/mi_qn4176/is_20060825/ai_n16700296> (September 8, 2007).

2. Herb Gould, "Right time, place for Patrick; Her attractiveness and popularity," Chicago Sun-Times, May 25, 2007, <http://findarticles.com/p/articles/mi_qn4155/is_20070525/ai_n19180027> (September 13, 2007).

3. Ibid.

4. Rux, August 25, 2006.

5. Nate Ryan, "For Patrick, the question has become: Can she win?" USA Today, May 23, 2007, <http://www.usatoday.com/sports/motor/irl/indy500/2007-05-23-danica-patrick_N.htm> (September 13, 2007).

6. Gould, May 25, 2007.

7. Ibid.

8. Ryan, May 23, 2007.

9. "Patrick wants to end Kournikova comparison," Yahoo.com, September 6, 2007, <http://news.yahoo.com/s/nm/20070907/sp_nm/motor_racing_patrick_dc> (September 13, 2007).

10. Ryan, May 23, 2007.

11. Ibid.

12. Chris Isidore, "Kournikova on wheels," CNNMoney.com, May 25, 2007, <http://money.cnn.com/2007/05/23/commentary/sportsbiz/index.htm> (September 13, 2007).

CHAPTER 9. THE ROLE MODEL AND MORE

1. Lya Wodraska, "Danica Patrick is a big sensation in IRL," The Salt Lake Tribune, May 26, 2006, <http://www.iwf.org/issues/issues_detail.asp?ArticleID=896> (September 20, 2007).

2. Dave Lewandowski, "Ready made role model," Indycar.com, June 19, 2005, <http://www.indycar.com/news/story.php?story_id=4873> (September 24, 2007).

3. Ibid.

4. Wodraska, May 26, 2006.

5. Ibid.

6. Brian Gomez, "All Eyes on Danica," The Gazette (Colorado

Springs), Aug. 17, 2005, <http://findarticles.com/p/articles/mi_qn4191/is_20050817/ai_n14918768/pg_1> (September 10, 2007).

7. "Rahal Letterman Racing Press Conference Transcript," Indy500.com, May 12, 2006, <http://www.indy500.com/news/story.php?story_id=6547> (September 12, 2007).

8. "Danica Patrick visits VCH," Vanderbiltchildrens.com, July 14, 2005, <http://www.vanderbiltchildrens.com/interior.php?mid=139&press_id=195> (September 26, 2007).

9. Ibid

10. Lewandowski, June 19, 2005.

CHAPTER 10. BREAKING THROUGH

1. Allan Brewer, "Danica Patrick Just One of the Guys at AGR," Fastmachines.com, March 7, 2007, <http://www.fastmachines.com/archives/irl/004148.php> (October 3, 2007).

2. Ibid.

3. "Danica Patrick Races into Town for Her Third Running in the Indianapolis 500," Indyschild.com, May 1, 2007, <http://www.indyschild.com/1editorialbody.lasso?-token.folder=2007-05-01&-token.story=191981.112112&-token.subpub> (September 29, 2007).

4. Brewer, March 7, 2007.

5. Ed Hinton, "Acting Has Vanished for Danica Patrick," The Orlando Sentinel, August 20, 2007, <http://www.theledger.com/apps/pbcs.dll/article?AID=/20070524/NEWS/705240548/0/FRONTPAGE> (September 8, 2007).

6. "Danica Patrick Races into Town for Her Third Running in the Indianapolis 500," Indyschild.com, May 1, 2007, <http://www.indyschild.com/1editorialbody.lasso?-token.folder=2007-05-01&-token.story=191981.112112&-token.subpub> (September 29, 2007).

7. Phillip B. Wilson, "Patrick's charge at Indy 500 interrupted," Indystar.com, May 28, 2007, <http://www.indystar.com/apps/pbcs.dll/article?AID=/20070528/SPORTS0101/705280402&theme> (September 19, 2007).

8. Ibid.

9. "Wheldon Shoved by Feisty Danica Patrick," Paddocktalk.com, June 4, 2007, <http://www.paddocktalk.com/news/html/modules.php?op=modload&name=News&file=article&sid=56991> (September 18, 2007).

10. "No fireworks between Danica, Wheldon as Hornish holds on for win," ESPN.com, June 10, 2007, <http://sports.espn.go.com/rpm/news/story?seriesId=1&id=2899370> (October 5, 2007).

11. Ibid.

12. "Danica Patrick Races into Town for Her Third Running in the Indianapolis 500," Indyschild.com, May 1, 2007, <http://www.indyschild.com/1editorialbody.lasso?-token.folder=2007-05-01&-token.story=191981.112112&-token.subpub> (September 29, 2007).

13. Nate Ryan, "Lady's first: Patrick revels in popular, historic win," USA Today, April 21, 2008, <http://www.usatoday.com/sports/motor/irl/2008-04-21-patrick-cover_N.htm> (September 20, 2008).

14. "Patrick triumphs in Japan, becomes first woman to win IndyCar race," ESPN.com, April 20, 2008, <http://sports.espn.go.com/rpm/racing/news/story?id=3355226> (September 20, 2008).

15. Ryan, April 21, 2008.

16. Ibid.

17. Ibid.

18. "Patrick triumphs in Japan, becomes first woman to win IndyCar race," ESPN.com, April 20, 2008, <http://sports.espn.go.com/rpm/racing/news/story?id=3355226> (September 20, 2008).

19. Dave Caldwell, "Racing to Victory, and Leaving the Men and the Doubters Behind," New York Times, April 21, 2008, <http://www.nytimes.com/2008/04/21/sports/othersports/21patrick.html?em&ex=1208836800&en=7e8cd1e5f575> (September 21, 2008).

20. Dave Albee, "Danica had bad days too," Marin Independent Journal, August 23, 2008, <http://www.marinij.com/sports/ci_10285815> (September 19, 2008).

21. David Goricki, "Patrick feeling fast on Belle Isle," The Detroit News, August 30, 2008, <http://www.detnews.com/apps/pbcs.dll/article?AID=/20080830/SPORTS03/808300356> (September 19, 2008).

22. Albee, August 23, 2008.

GLOSSARY

air pressure—The amount of air in a tire measured in pounds per cubic inch.

Barber Dodge Pro Series—Formerly a part of the CART series, drivers race in identical cars.

caution flag (yellow flag)—Waved when drivers are required to slow down due to an accident or other hazard on the track.

Championship Auto Racing Teams (CART)—Formerly the top open-wheel racing series in the United States. CART changed its name to Champ Car World Series in 2004.

checkered flag—The flag that is waved as the winner of a race crosses the start/finish line.

crew—The members of a racing team who help build and repair cars either at the team's shop or at the track during race weekend.

crew chief—The manager of a race team who oversees the mechanics of the car and the crew and is responsible for their performance on race day.

go-kart—A small vehicle with a motor that fits one person. Many of the world's top racers got their start in go-kart racing, which is called karting.

green flag—Signals the start of a race, a restart after a caution, a qualification session, or a practice session.

Indy Racing League—One of the top open-wheel racing circuits in the United States. IRL drivers race on both oval tracks and road tracks throughout North America.

lap—One trip around the track.

open-wheel racing—Race cars that do not have fenders. The Indy Racing League, Formula One, and Champ Car World Series feature open-wheel racing.

pit road—The area where pit crews service the cars, usually along the front straightaway.

podium—The stage or platform where the top three finishers in a race stand after a race to receive their trophies and other awards.

points standings—A list that shows how many points each driver has accumulated during a season. Points are awarded based on where a driver finishes a race.

qualifying—A process in which cars are timed in laps on the track by themselves. The fastest cars get to start in the best positions for a race.

FOR MORE INFORMATION

WEB LINKS

Danica Patrick's Web site:
www.danicaracing.com

IndyCar Series Web site:
www.indycar.com

World Karting Association's Web site:
www.worldkarting.com

FURTHER READING

Baukus Mello, Tara. *Danica Patrick*. New York: Chelsea House Publishers, 2008.

Indy-Tech Publishing Editorial Staff. *Danica Patrick*. Indianapolis, Ind.: Indy-Tech Publishing, 2006.

Patrick, Danica, with Laura Morton. *Danica: Crossing the Line*. New York: Simon and Schuster, 2006.